How I Managed $20,000,000,000.00 by Age 32

Wade W. Slome, CFA, CFP®

Dedicated in memory of my brother, Todd S. Slome, whose life provided purpose and inspiration.
And to my wonderful wife, Robin, and magnificent munchkins, Whitney & Hayley.

Table of Contents

Preface

How I Managed $20,000,000,000.00 by Age 32 was designed to provide a unique peek into the mind of an experienced fund manager who has managed large pools of money - through the best of times and the worst of times. In order to present a proper perspective on my investment career, I intend to describe a diverse set of personal and professional experiences that have shaped my belief systems. Another key purpose of this book is to equip readers with a new set of investment strategies and tools that will assist investors in achieving a higher level of financial success.

I have enjoyed an incredible run thus far and I hope you will join me in reliving these exceptional experiences in the following pages.

Sincerely,

Wade W. Slome

Wade W. Slome, CFA, CFP®

Chapter 1: Influences/The Beginning

Introduction

What a wild ride it has been. From trading penny stocks in high school stock market competitions after the '1987 Crash' to trading billions of dollars whilst elbowing with the likes of Eric Schmidt (CEO of Google), Jeff Bezos (CEO of Amazon), and John Chambers (CEO of Cisco Systems)...I have seen it all. There is no playbook for managing billions of dollars, starting your own investment firm, and running a hedge fund. My life story has been rather circuitous, taking me everywhere from California to New York and from Australia to China along the way. I even took a nine year pit-stop in America's heartland, where I managed a $20,000,000,000.00 fund at American Century Investments. As a freshly minted MBA grad from Cornell University in 1998, I never expected in my wildest dreams to land on one of the 10 biggest funds in the country. America, what a great place to live! My journey eventually sucked me back towards the Pacific Ocean, where I now lead my investment practice in Newport Beach, California. The opening of 'market' trading hours at 6:30 a.m. is not ideal out here on the West Coast, but sleep is overrated – I can rest in the afterlife.

I view investing as a combination of art and science. Too much emphasis on either aspect can be very detrimental to investors' financial health. In the late 1990s, art manifested itself in the form of a greedy general public (the herd) piling into technology stocks near the peak of the market, only to capitulate into panicked sales close to the market bottom in 2002. More recently, the bursting of the housing bubble has proven the herd will never fully satisfy its appetite for greed or adequately manage the volatile swings of fear. I too have staggered along with the herd and journeyed with the pack off a few cliffs in my day. Fortunately, I have grown from these lessons and have come to realize the grass is greener and the eating more plentiful off the herd's beaten path.

I consider the science of investing a disciplined process that successful investors consistently use as a guiding light, no matter the actual or perceived pressures that are impacting the market. Some renowned investors have married the art and science facets into time-tested winning strategies. We will explore and discuss numerous success stories, including those of astute growth investors like William O'Neil, Phil Fisher, Peter Lynch, and other sage experts. For example, Lynch successfully managed the Fidelity Magellan Fund from 1977 to 1990 and averaged a 29% annual return. During that period the S&P 500 index generated a 15% annualized return. Lynch recognized that investment success doesn't come easily when he explained, "Investing is 99% perspiration." For instance, in 1986, Mr. Lynch visited 200 companies in just one year and read 700 Annual Reports. A lot can be learned from the triumphs and failures of others.

Over the years, I have spent loads of laboratory time testing and tweaking numerous investment theories and hypotheses. In tying together the art with the science, whether through intensive interviews with a company CFO or through picking apart a quantitative model or cash-flow statement, I believe a common sense approach trumps all other approaches. As Warren Buffett says, "Invest in what you know." Plain old common sense has served as my preeminent compass in guiding me toward my investment successes. When analyzing a stock or investment I have a never-ending voice in my head that skips like a scratched record, constantly asking me such questions as: "Does this make sense? Is this data consistent with all the other information I gathered? If not, why?" Management teams are notoriously good at smoothly marketing their products, services and strategies. So at the end of the day, if it sounds too good to be true, then it likely is. There are no free lunches in the stock market or, as I see it, in any form of investing. Savings accounts generally do not yield 10%, and there is a reason for that – the depositor is assuming lower relative risk as compared to most alternative investments. Earning higher returns requires the assumption of additional risk. Sure there is a minority of talented investment professionals that can earn excess returns ("alpha") over the long-run. However a diligent, consistent process that merges art/science is required.

But I did not grow up in the investing laboratory – I was shaped by many experiences and influences before I ended up on the path of a successful professional investor. On the topic of 'success' I agree with philosopher Albert Schweitzer, who said, "Success is not the key to happiness. Happiness is the key to

success. If you love what you are doing, you will be successful."
I strive to lead my life with these words in mind.

The Beginning

I grew up in a fairly ordinary middle-class neighborhood in a suburb of the San Francisco Bay Area...Fremont, California. From a very young age I had an entrepreneurial interest in business. Beyond the normal adolescent paper route, I also engineered a Reese's chocolate & peanut butter confection business in 5th grade with the help of my good friend, Steve Emerson, and worked my way up to stock market competitions in high school. *The Wall Street Journal* turned out to be a staple in my life; but even back then, I had no clue where my professional future would take me.

Motivation was never in short supply. All I had to do was glance over at my mother, who successfully raised three boys from diapers through college while working full-time, a widow at the ripe young age of 35. (My dad passed away in 1970.) My mother poured her sweat and tears into her job as a mechanical draftswoman in the engineering department of a large publicly traded trucking company. Only after clocking out of a long, hard day of work, did she have the luxury of coming home to three screaming kids that had to be bathed, fed, educated, and comforted - along with all the other needs children demand.

I did not know my father, Herb Slome, very well given the fact that I was only five months old when he passed away. As a young man, my dad excelled in academics. While in high school, his academic achievements were recognized through newspaper clippings and radio show appearances. This success continued into college. He proceeded to receive an academic scholarship to the University of Pittsburgh, earned Phi Beta Kappa membership, and graduated with the distinction of Magna Cum Laude. Despite Jewish admission quotas, my father conquered the bitter odds and over time graduated from medical school at the University of Pittsburgh. In 1962, he completed his medical internship at the University of California, San Francisco, and became a pediatrician in the San Francisco Bay Area.

My mother, Ruth (maiden name Lorenz), was born in Germany and met my father while he served as a doctor on an American Air Force base in Germany (Rhein Main). Although German is not considered "the language of love", my father endured a few private German language lessons while falling in love and the rest is history. After my parents married in Germany, my father returned to the States, finished his pediatric internship and eventually started his practice.

From an outsider's perspective one might think my parents would mix like oil and vinegar. Never mind that my father was brought up Jewish, and my grandfather on my mother's side worked for the Nazis (mandatorily). I suppose my father could not complain about religious consistency across family borders because he himself converted to Zen Buddhism before he passed away. Former philosopher and divinity guru Alan Watts was a staple of his spiritual diet even though my dad grew up in temples and went to the Jewish equivalent of the YMCA, called the YMHA (Young Men's Hebrew Association). My great grandfather on my dad's side lived in Lithuania. Add the fact that my mother was a practicing New Apostolic (a German offshoot of Catholicism with approximately 11 million members globally), and the result was a very eclectic family unit to say the least. When I try to explain my family heritage, friends usually don't believe me or they just think I belonged to a cult. Eventually they give me the benefit of the doubt, and I allay their concerns by not shaving my head or growing a ponytail.

With my father passing on at a young age, my mother was left to pick up the pieces and was forced to maintain the family unity. Believe it or not, the strict German values instilled into me and my two brothers had some advantages. Hard will, discipline, manners, determination, and respect for others were drilled into our heads at a very young age. Overall, I did my best to stay out of trouble and ease my mother's child-herding burdens; nonetheless I couldn't completely escape the wrath of the 'discipline-belt' or the fury of 'woody', the spanking spoon. Behavior modification was the main goal and these modification techniques were generally effective despite today's beliefs in softer obedience strategies like 'cuddle and converse'. The lessons derived from my upbringing unquestionably contributed to my future educational and professional successes. Even though I hated discipline at the time, there are certain grueling stock market environments that have mentally scarred me worse than any dreaded wooden spoon drubbings.

Growing up Bavarian style did, however, have its drawbacks beyond the valuable lessons I learned. Lederhosen were one major downside. As the youngest of three boys, I had two future generations of stiff, smelly, chaffing leather shorts to look forward to. After I grew out of one pair, my elder brothers were more than happy to pass the lederhosen baton down to me so I could set more groundbreaking fashion trends. Needless to say, running around the playground in leather shorts is not the most comfortable attire, not to mention that leather is not the most cleaner-friendly material either.

Aside from growing up wearing strange German clothing, I also grew up with a peculiar surname too - Slome. Not S-a-l-a-m-i, not S-l-o-a-n, not S-l-o-m-e-e, but rather S-L-O-M-E (rhymes with 'home'). The origin of the Slome name has a unique backdrop. Apparently, the Slome name was initially derived from the name Slomavitz, going back to my father's descendants in Lithuania. In order to become more American-ized or out of pure laziness, upon emigrating to the United States of America, my Slomavitz descendants decided to chop off the "-vitz" and transform the name to "Slome". I can think of some superior names, but I have to admit that I am partial to the name 'Slome' over 'Slomavitz'!

Another aspect of my upbringing that affected my investment career is my extreme inner-competitiveness. Whether during a casual game of Scrabble with my in-laws or a professional discussion over the discount rate used in a stock's discounted cash flow model, I despise losing. Discipline did not only come from the determination passed on by my mother, but also through my intense passion and competitive love for sports.

My childhood sports addictions centered on soccer, baseball, and basketball – in that order. My hobbies of tennis and golf blossomed later on in life; but as single player sports, these areas never gained the same level of appeal to me as team sports. The camaraderie I developed through team-based sports was a function of common sacrifices performed for the purpose of reaching a common goal. These friendships, in many instances, have transcended time from childhood to adulthood. One cannot put a price tag on these life-long sporting lessons that were cultivated from failure, success, discipline, and plain old hard work.

Although I consider myself a B- overall athletically, my Andy Warhol 15 minutes of fame came shortly after I received a call from my friend, Andy Pierce, in the late 1980s. "Hey Slome, there's a few walk-on spots open at the Stanford basketball camp…wanna go?" he cautiously inquired. This camp was an intensive multi-day camp that targeted talented college recruits and was run by Cardinal Coach (and eventual NBA Head Coach) Michael Montgomery. As walk-ons, we were treated as second-class citizens, and few of the assistants or supporting coaches had any clue who we were. Well, they quickly learned who Wade Slome (a.k.a. Darth Wader) was after I obliterated the large field of talented college recruits with my raining outside jumpers, my surgically penetrating dribble drives, and my clamp down defense that would have even made Gary "the Glove" Payton proud.

Moments like these were uncommon; however these types of events can even occur in the investing world. One occasionally enters a zone – a state of nirvana – experienced in similar fashion as professional athletes and employees. When you are in that 'zone' you basically can do no wrong. After a very brief trophy and t-shirt ceremony and a call back to my school to unearth my measly offensive statistics, the Stanford staff indeed learned that my success was a fluke. Being a celebrity was entertaining while it lasted, but I may have been better served by calling Woody Harrelson for a cameo spot in his movie, "White Men Can't Jump." Although my skill level occasionally has been questioned, this event epitomizes how the mind can triumph over matter when determination removes artificially, self-created barriers.

My athletic genes certainly did not come from my dad, who was more in his element with a book in hand rather than a football. Almost all of dad's hard cover books were classics - from Marcus Aurelius to John Paul Sartre; from Stendahl to Dostoyevski; from Poe to Hemingway; from Faulkner to Cheever; from Shakespeare to the sayings of Buddha. On the other hand, my mother was an accomplished gymnast and overall first-class athlete.

Ironically my dad, whose occupation was to improve his patients' health, had a heart attack after a health-motivated jog around the neighborhood. Life is too short and I do not take it for granted. Whether it is taking on the responsibility of managing a multi-billion dollar fund or the simple pleasure of holding my daughter's hand while at the beach, each experience and relationship that I have built upon will only make my life richer and more fulfilling. The world of investing is an ever-changing dynamic game that absolutely satisfies my urge to face new challenges. Anyone who has invested over multiple economic cycles realizes that the market has a way of humbling you. If one does not respect the market's powers and authority, then 'Mr. Market' will find a way to bludgeon you over the head with a sledgehammer.

Another passion that permeates through my lens of life is my love for travel. Over the last four decades I have had the opportunity to travel through 25 countries on five continents. I firmly believe that my travels, meetings and discussions that have accumulated over my lifetime have led me to become a better stock market investor. The market is an explosive mixture between art and science. The art aspects rely heavily on the appreciation of people's behavior and how they react to fear and greed. What better way to gain a clearer perspective about people's behavior and their ride on the unstoppable freight train of "globalization" than by meeting people firsthand from all over the world? I will dig deeper into the topic of globalization later in this book.

My passion for competitive sports intersected with my love of travel when I committed to climbing Mt. Whitney, the tallest mountain in the lower 48 states of the United States - the peak stands at about 14,500 feet. Bloomberg News profiled my ascent in 2005 (see Appendix) when I in fact completed the round-trip climb in 11 ½ hours, some three less hours than expected. I am constantly pushing myself towards new challenges both in my personal and professional life. When it comes to investing, the market is constantly evolving. As a portfolio manager, in order to grow professionally and respond to those evolutions, I need to constantly push myself out of my comfort zone. As Mario Andretti, the only driver ever to win the Indianapolis 500 (1969), the Daytona 500 (1967), and the Formula One World Championship, said: "If everything's under control, you're going too slow." Just as I was out of my comfort area when I climbed Mt. Whitney, I also try to escape my comfort zone in my professional life. Whether researching the science behind the efficacy of a biotech drug marketed by Genentech (DNA), or navigating through the technical specs of a new semiconductor chip for Qualcomm's (QCOM) CDMA chips, I have never struggled in unearthing new challenging concepts to push my personal envelope. I continually repeat this mantra to myself.

Isolated, my background experiences and influences may seem trivial. However, in totality, they have had a dramatic impact in how I reflect on the world of finance and investing. Without discipline, there could be no successful process. Without motivation, investment opportunities would continually slip through the cracks. Without respect and integrity, there would be no relationships to build information networks. Discipline, determination, and integrity instilled into me through my tight association of family and friends have created a foundation necessary to achieve my dreams and goals, including the dream of managing a $20,000,000,000 fund by the age of 32.

Chapter 2: No Success without
Failure / Paying My Dues

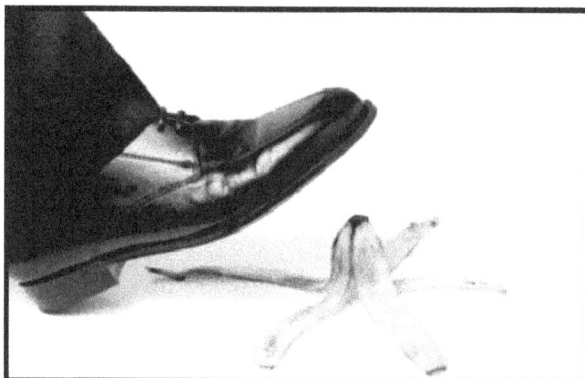

No pain, no gain. Life has a way of throwing you curve balls. I've swung and struck out, gotten hit by pitches and even missed the bus to the baseball game. But in order to get into the batter's box to hit that game winning home run in the majors, you first have to work your way up through the minor leagues and take a lot of swings.

Cruis-ing Along

My AAA farm-team journey started as an intern in 1992 at Oppenheimer & Co. as an assistant to stock broker, Tom Kreuzer (pronounced Cruise-er but he wasn't married to Katie Holmes). I thought Lincoln had abolished slavery, but because I wanted to get my feet wet and I had an interest in stocks, I volunteered to intern for free...yes, that's right, I collected no booty.

I enjoyed the 5% of stock talk and I learned a ton for a part-time college job, but 95% of my time was devoted to sales and cold calls, which wasn't what I had originally envisioned for the position when I first signed up. With a phone receiver stuck to my head, I was not a happy camper sifting through the pages of the Beverly Hills phone book calling seniors like Myrtle Jones and asking, "Mrs. Jones, are you happy with your investments? Well, my name is Wade Slome and I am calling from Oppenheimer & Company. We have an incredible 6% coupon California Orange County Municipal bond yielding 9.25%." If the old ladies had not already hung up on me by that point, I briskly handed the call off to Mr. Kreuzer, "the Schmoozer", to work his sales magic.

There are plenty of good stock brokers, but after a few thousand cold-calls, I gained a new found appreciation for advancing my educational career and realized I wanted to broaden my investment career aspirations. Although it may have been my most dreaded job, this employment experience may have proved to be the most invaluable of my career. Very few careers or professions lead to success without the artful skill of salesmanship, whether you are talking about doctors, lawyers, sculptors, or even the fry-guy at McDonalds. Regardless, if someone is selling an idea to a superior or promoting a product to a consumer, the better one is at selling the more successful one will be in their professional career over time.

Life as a Banker

From the stock brokerage industry, I moved on to investment banking as an intern at E. J. De La Rosa & Co. – a minority-owned investment bank that assisted in raising financing for municipal projects ranging from hospitals and stadiums to roadways and refinancings. I again wedged my foot in the door by offering my services for no cost…ughh. In due time my contributions were recognized and I began receiving what seemed like fat paychecks for a starving student at the time. For a youngster at UCLA to learn basic time value of money cash flow models, along with accounting concepts of debits and credits was hugely insightful. While working as an undergraduate student, I also audited a graduate course in Finance with Professor Robert Geske. I was not putting the MBA students to shame, but the introduction to Modern Portfolio Theory and asset pricing models such as CAPM (Capital Asset Pricing Model) and Black & Scholes (options valuation) helped to broaden my perspective on how investment management concepts tied in with retail brokerage and investment banking practices.

Although my experience at De La Rosa led to full-time opportunities and interviews on Wall Street at Kidder Peabody, Lehman Brothers, Merrill Lynch, and what was formerly Bear Stearns (among others), my I-banking position served its purpose as a tremendous stepping stone. Banking is great, but this experience clarified my career ambitions, which was investing in stocks.

Introduction to a Stock Addiction (William O'Neil & Co.)

Buying a share in a stock – actually owning a portion of a company while holding voting rights - has tremendous allure. Besides the intellectual appeal, the more primal aspects of trading the stock market fascinated me. I am an adrenaline junky and committing cold, hard-earned cash towards personal investments got my blood pumping (and still does). Markets are constantly changing, and you get report cards daily as stock quotes measure your performance persistently. Reading books is fantastic, but I strongly believe there is no better way to learn than by just simply diving in.

My worst mistakes and best lessons came from my early trading days in my first post-college job. Sir John Templeton, the great global investor, stated: "The big difference between those who are successful and those who are not, is that the successful people learn from their mistakes and the mistakes of others." Throughout my investment career, I have maintained a process to objectively analyze my mistakes and the reason(s) for them. "If a man didn't make mistakes he'd own the world in a month. But if he didn't profit by his mistakes he wouldn't own a blessed thing," maintained famed trader, Jesse Livermore. This is a humbling profession, and unlike sports professionals, this is a field that learning and experience will only help over decades – you don't need to flame out in your 20s or 30s like some professional athletes.

My first real taste of investing, outside of stock competitions, came after college. My investment banking experience gained at E. J. De La Rosa & Company, crystallized my professional purpose. I love stocks. With this in mind, I was ecstatic when I saw the posting for research analyst at William O'Neil & Co. on the UCLA job board at the career center. Better yet, my friend,

Mike Kerrane, from my UCLA fraternity (Sigma Phi Epsilon), worked there.

William O'Neil is a tremendous investor…and entrepreneur. He was born in Oklahoma and raised in Texas. One of his claims to fame was that his portfolio experienced a 20 fold increase in 26 months. His company, William O'Neil & Company, was formed in 1963 and led to the creation of his newspaper, *Investor's Business Daily* (IBD) in 1984. This was a way for Bill O'Neil to face the "Goliath" of a monopoly (*The Wall Street Journal*) and punch them in the eye. Another perk of the job was that I would be working with some great hotshot investors like David Ryan (winner of national investing contests) and Lee Freestone, a young protégé of Bill O'Neil.

The job as a research analyst was not the most glamorous but the lessons were life lasting. Squished into tiny cubicles packed together, I was not initially given a telephone – a telephone was something to be earned once your dedication was proven after months of hard work (ultimately I landed one!). In 1993, before mass-data internet downloads were available, we manually input stock data through our keyboard terminals into massive mainframe computers. Besides entering text from annual reports and government filings (10Ks & 10Qs), we also input lots of quarterly sales and earnings data from corporate press releases.

If monkey work was all we did, I might have just shot myself. The incredible aspect of the job was that management encouraged stock trading, even during work hours! Over time, I found my physical stamina improving dramatically as I shuttled back and forth from my cozy cubicle to the hot action of the Quotron stock quote machine at the other side of the research room. I constantly checked on my portfolio, along with stock prospects I had researched through the tools provided by William O'Neil. O'Neil's philosophy, which significantly shapes my views today, is based on his concept C-A-N-S-L-I-M. The main components of his philosophy are the following:

- **Current Earnings:** In his book, *How to Make Money in Stocks*, Mr. O'Neil states, "I would suggest you not buy any stock that doesn't show earnings per share up at least 18 or 20% in the most recent quarter." Basically he believes that if you want to encounter superior stock returns, you will need to find those companies with superior earnings growth rates.

- **Annual Earnings:** Mr. O'Neil goes on to say, "The annual compounded growth rate of earnings in the superior firms you hand pick for purchasing stock in should be from 15 to 50%, or even more, per year."

- **New Product, Service, or Change:** In order to make outsized returns, Mr. O'Neil directs investors towards companies that have new products, new management teams, new services, or are experiencing new industry changes. If there is nothing new, the stock price is likely accounting for future prospects.

- **Supply and Demand:** When considering different stocks, Mr. O'Neil argues that superior returns are achieved by concentrating on those companies that have a lower "supply" of shares outstanding, thereby in a sense creating a scarcity value for those stock shares.

- **Leader or Laggard:** Simply put, Mr. O'Neil expresses, "It seldom pays to invest in laggard performing stocks even if they look tantalizingly cheap. Look for the market leader."

- **Institutional Sponsorship:** It takes a lot of buying demand to significantly drive up the price of a stock. Mr. O'Neil passionately believes that that institutional sponsorship (ownership) is a key ingredient to move prices higher.

- **Market Indexes:** O'Neil centers attention on the broader market perspective too: "You can be right on every one of the first 6 factors *(C-A-N-S-L-I-M)*; however, if you are wrong about the direction of the broad general market, three out of four of your stocks will slump with the market averages and you will lose money...You do not need to know what the market is going to do! All you need to know is what the market has actually done!"

After my C-A-N-S-L-I-M indoctrination, I felt ready to invest. Before long I had my margin account open and began actively trading stocks and options. Unfortunately, my biotech miracle stock, Saliva Diagnostics (SALV), did not take off to the moon and provide a retirement opportunity at age 21. On the surface it sounded brilliant. Spit in a cup and this diagnostic test would let you know whether you have HIV. With the millions of HIV/AIDS patients around the world, the profit potential behind 'Saliva' was virtually limitless. The technology unfortunately did not quite pan out; however, it was mistakes like these that formed scars which would help shape the foundations of my successful investing career.

After cutting my teeth at William O'Neil & Co., I had grander ambitions. I started and passed the first two levels of the CFA (Chartered Financial Analyst Program) examination, an intensive three-year program with a focus on finance and investments. Like most masochists who decided to take these series of exams, I was a glutton for punishment and put my life on hold for a few years. As you can see the pass rates are extremely competitive:

CFA EXAM PASS RATES

Year	Level I	Level II	Level III
2008	35%	46%	53%
2007	39%	40%	50%
2006	40%	48%	76%
2005	35%	56%	55%
2004	35%	32%	64%
2003	41%	47%	68%
2002	44%	47%	58%
2001	49%	46%	82%
2000	52%	54%	65%

Far Above Cayuga's Waters

But why stop there? Why not study and take the GMAT exam as well, so that I could apply to business school? I knew I wanted to be a fund manager and most asset management positions were back East, with the rare exception of a few larger firms like American Funds/Capital Research, Franklin-Templeton, PIMCO, and Nicholas-Applegate. Cornell University turned out to be an ideal location between Wall Street (New York City) and State Street (Boston), home of Fidelity and hundreds of billions of assets under management. I went there, as legendary bank robber, Willie Sutton, famously quipped, "because that's where all the money is." Ithaca, situated in the rolling hills of upstate New York above Cayuga Lake, also served as an ideally secluded environment to take advantage of Cornell's premier finance, investment, and accounting courses, taught by top-notch professors like Charles M. C. Lee and Bhaskaran 'Swami' Swaminathan. Their enthusiastic teaching styles were contagious and sucked in broad student interest – and given Swami's ties to UCLA, you knew he was a smart cookie.

But Cornell was not all roses and chocolates. I had a leg up over most of my job-searching competitors due to my CFA experience and my investment background at William O'Neil & Co.; however these "buy-side" jobs were generally more highly sought-after than the more abundant "sell-side" grinder positions. Getting a job on the sell-side focused a bit more on selling products and services than the actual investing aspects of the stock market. The "buy-side" premium on investment management positions meant that I was competing with lots of candidates from Harvard, Wharton, Stanford, and Chicago. As time passed, I learned that I could more than hold my own; and before long, I was flying all around the country - from Fidelity to Janus, Invesco to Capital Group.

I eventually scored an incredible summer internship at Nicholas-Applegate ($32 billion in assets under management at the time) in their penthouse offices that overlooked the Pacific Ocean from downtown San Diego. Glamorous internships on $4 billion small cap growth funds, like the fund I was assigned, meant that my services could only be attained at a towering cost -- $5.15 per hour to be exact (the going minimum wage at the time in 1997).

My mission to internship employment was not fully accomplished, however, until I had accumulated what I describe as the sprawling "Wall of Shame." Imagine if you will, a three-walled room in a 700 square foot apartment, and in this study room you discover endless numbers of ruffled sheets of 'rejection letters' that climb two of the sidewalls to form an endless stream of neutral-colored wallpaper. These form-letters were almost comical in their approaches. Some did little to beat around the bush – "we have found a more qualified candidate." Others would attempt to soften the blow by explaining, "we will keep your resume on file in the event a future opening will arise." Or some fund companies were just plain lazy, either using the rubber-stamped signature or simply neglecting to include a signature.

There was, however, a silver lining to all this doom and denunciation. After accumulating dozens of these rejection badges, little did I know that these sheets of paper were worth their weight in gold (or beer). Come graduation week, the local tavern, Jonny O's, decided out of pity and compassion to honor each job applicant's rejection letter as a free beer coupon. Good thing that through all that studying I had built up quite a thirst. Let's hope for Al Gore's sake, that Jonny O's recycles – it would be a shame to see all that paper go to waste!

Lessons Learned

Professionally, I have made plenty of mistakes too. Many of my investment mistakes have been tied to roll-up or acquisition-reliant growth stories, where the allure of rapid growth shielded the underlying weak fundamentals of the core businesses. I have drunk the Kool-Aid of several "story" stocks during the technology bubble days too – for example, Webvan (a grocery delivery concept). How could mixing Domino's pizza delivery with Wal-Mart's low-priced goods NOT work? I'm just lazy enough to demand a service like that! Well, after spending hundreds of millions of dollars and never reaching the scale necessary to cover the razor thin profit margins, Webvan folded up operations. But don't give up hope yet, Amazon is refocusing its attention on the grocery space (mostly non-perishables now) and could become the dominant food delivery retailer. Fortunately for me, and other professionals, one does not need to be right all the time to outperform the indices. "If you're terrific in this business you're right 6 times out of 10 – I've had stocks go from $11 to 7 cents (American Intl Airways)," admitted Peter Lynch. Growth investing expert, Phil Fisher, added:

"Fortunately the long-range profits earned from really good common stocks should more than balance the losses from a normal percentage of such mistakes."

As you can see from my experiences, I have swung at quite a few pitches and missed my fair share of them. But it is clear to me that you cannot hit a home run if you do not step into the batter's box and take a big cut at that occasional fat pitch floating above the plate. If somebody wants to consider me a failure, then great, I am following in the footsteps of Abraham Lincoln – an epitome of failure and facing adversity. Not only did Lincoln fail as a businessman (he operated a failed general store), but he also witnessed the deaths of two young sons, experienced defeat twice as a Senatorial and Congressional candidate, faced loss as a Vice Presidential candidate, only to go on to become one of the greatest Presidents of all-time. Amazing.

Warren Buffett takes a more light-hearted approach when he describes mistakes and failure: "If you were a golfer and you had a hole in one on every hole, the game wouldn't be any fun. At least that's my explanation of why I keep hitting them in the rough." With that said, I'm off to the golf course…fore!

Chapter 3: Chasing Profits – Is the Market Efficient?

The Efficiency Question

The answer to the key question relating to whether the market is efficient is central in determining how one should invest his money. If you believe the market is purely efficient, then dial 1-800-VANGUARD and buy some index funds. If you believe the market is inefficient, then invest in an exploitable strategy or hire an active investment manager you believe can outperform the market after fees and taxes.

I will review some of the compelling evidence on both sides of the ledger. In the end, I fall somewhere in between both sides of the argument. Like the scarce number of .300 hitters in baseball, I believe there are a select few investment managers who can consistently outperform the market. In 2007, AssociatedContent.com did a study that showed there were only 12 active career .300 hitters in Major League Baseball. In John Bogle's *Common Sense on Mutual Funds*, he argues the probabilities of a mutual fund beating an index over the long haul is less than one in four - a plethora of academic research supports this assertion.

Richard Roll, one of the gurus of the efficient market hypothesis, said this: "I have personally tried to invest money, my client's and my own, in every single anomaly and predictive result that academics have dreamed up. And I have yet to make a nickel on any of these supposed market inefficiencies. An inefficiency ought to be an exploitable opportunity. If there's nothing investors can exploit in a systematic way, time in and time out, then it's very hard to say that information is not being properly incorporated into stock prices. Real money investment strategies

don't produce the results that academic papers say they should."
(*Wall Street Journal*, 12/28/00)

Efficient Market Hypothesis (EMH):

The Efficient Market Hypothesis theory states that consistent excess returns CANNOT be achieved because the market is efficient and reflects all available information.

The EMH was developed in large part by Professor Eugene Fama, from the University of Chicago Graduate School of Business, as a result of research he did in the 1960s. The theory was popularized by Burton Malkiel, a renowned economist and professor at Princeton University, through his best-selling book, *A Random Walk Down Wall Street*. In the novel he evangelizes on the power of passive index fund investing and critically evaluates the merits of technical analysis (seeking profits through chart patterns) and fundamental analysis (analysis of financial statements, industry dynamics, management teams, etc). John Bogle, the driving force behind the Vanguard Group, built his company off the principles of the EMH. As a positive consequence of this concerted strategy, Mr. Bogle has grown Vanguard's assets under management to well over $1 trillion.

The evolution of the EMH has created numerous interpretations and therefore has manifested itself into multiple forms. Here are the basic camps that academics have lumped EMH:

- **Random Walk**: This form of EMH states that stock price changes are unpredictable and cannot be exploited.
- **Weak Form of EMH** (Technical Analysis reflected in price): Prices reflect all PUBLICLY available data (i.e. price, volume, and other published info). Excess returns can however be earned from Fundamental Analysis and Inside Information.
- **Semi-strong Form EMH** (Technical & Fundamental Analysis reflected in price): Price reflects all historical data PLUS financial information (financial statements), industry data, and macroeconomic inputs. Excess returns can ONLY be achieved through inside information.
- **Strong Form EMH** (Technical & Fundamental Analysis reflected in price): Price reflects all public and PRIVATE information (Inside Information) – even insiders cannot outperform the market consistently. This is the most extreme view of the EMH.

Most Wall Street professionals cannot dispute a lot of the EMH data because the evidence is very compelling that the vast majority of professional money managers significantly underperform passive forms of investing (i.e. index funds). If push were to come to shove, I would likely fall into the 'Weak Form' of the EMH. It's safe to say that most of Wall Street falls into this camp, because if they didn't believe professionals could outperform the market, they would virtually have no product or service to hawk and they would be unemployed. Having said that, I believe there are only a small percentage of investors that have the capability of earning excess returns through the implementation of fundamental analysis and/or quantitative analysis. There are a relatively few hitters in Major League Baseball that can consistently achieve above a .300 batting average. I believe the same principle applies to investing.

Stronger form EMH disciples have a very difficult time explaining the long term excess returns by the likes of Fidelity Investments' Peter Lynch who managed the Magellan Fund from 1977 – 1990 and averaged a 29% annual return vs. a 15% return for the S&P 500 index. Warren Buffett is another investing standout that cannot rationally be explained. How does one rationalize the incredible 15 year streak that Bill Miller of Legg Mason attained in beating the S&P 500 Index? Statistical anomaly? Perhaps not. Lots of academic research points to the "Law of Large Numbers" leading to these aberrations. Or in other words, the market is statistically due to create some of these "Super Investors" out of the woodwork purely out of random chance.

In addition, how do strong EMH-ers explain the 1987 Crash, when the S&P 500 index fell 25% in one day? If all information in the market is accounted for in current stock prices, then how can investors experience such a large drop in stock prices over such a short duration? We can go much further back in time too. How was the "Tulip-mania" bubble that burst in the mid 17th Century justified under this framework?

A more recent example of irrational inefficiency can be evaluated via the study of the 1990s technology boom. The mid-to-late 1990s were jubilant times with many lemmings, day-traders, and casual investors chasing technology stocks and the hottest 5-star funds du jour, only to see their fortunes shattered in the wake of the 'New Economy' demise. "Paradigm shifts," "B2B & B2C models," "sticky eyeballs," "dot-com convergence," "frictionless growth" and "bricks-to-clicks" were all raging terms of the day. Cab drivers and barbers confidently recommended sure-fire stock tips, with names like Commerce One, Lucent Technologies, Ariba Inc., along with the "Four Horsemen" of technology, Cisco Systems, Sun Microsystems, Oracle Corp., and EMC Corp. who achieved combined market valuation of about $1.2 trillion at the zenith of the NASDAQ market. Needless to say, many of these stocks imploded in value by 80-90% over the subsequent months and years, before eventually stabilizing or capitulating into survival-based mergers. The Roman Candle-like trajectory of the market returns in the late 1990s and the early 2000s has shown how extreme the pendulum can swing towards greed and fear in different psychological stages of the market.

Real Estate Excesses

Well, let us not forget about the recent real estate bubble either. We humans are mighty resilient in our quest to find instant-wealth gratification or get-rich-quick schemes. So like frogs, the public decided to jump from one "bubble" lily pad (Technology) to another (Real Estate). The estimated and growing trillions in expected mortgage losses triggered by the gluttonous behavior in the subprime housing market (approximately 6 million subprime loans outstanding) has left investors picking up the pieces in search of the next bubble. According to Mortimer Zuckerman, *US News & World Report* journalist, there are ten million houses "upside down" (mortgage value exceeds asset value) and the number is increasing dramatically. To put these losses in perspective, let's not forget that the global GDP (Gross Domestic Product) engine churns out about $60 trillion in products and services annually.

So how did our major U.S. investment banks disintegrate (Bear Stearns & Lehman Brothers), our gargantuan mortgage financers Fannie Mae and Freddie Mac vanish from public markets, and how did trillions of dollars disintegrate from the balance sheets of Washington Mutual, AIG (American International Group, Inc.), Merrill Lynch and other financial institutions? Like most bubble-icious recipes, there is a healthy dose of greed, mixed with fear, sprinkled with loose and/or faulty regulation. The number of banks in our country contributed to this jam too. Over the last 25 years or so we have seen the price of credit steadily cheapen until recently. With very low barriers to entry we experienced an explosion in the number of banks. Ronald

Masulis, a professor at Vanderbilt, predicted the 15,000 banks that existed in 1990 would be reduced to only 4,500 banks, primarily driven by consolidation and the need for cost savings and economies of scale. Of late that number has come down due to rising bank failures – not mergers. The S&L (Savings and Loan) Crisis of the late-1980s and early-1990s was a period with many of the same cross-currents we are seeing in today's current mortgage crisis, originally triggered by destructive subprime lending tactics. During the period from 1986-1995, the number of federally insured Savings and Loan institutions fell from 3,234 to 1,645. Cleaning up the mess from all these bubbles is always painful, and in 1991 Congress pulled out the Hoover vacuum cleaner with its $78 billion bailout package for the Savings & Loans (S&L) companies. The 2008 approved $700 billion Troubled Asset Relief Program (TARP) shows the severity of this most recent credit crisis.

Also endemic of the early 1900s was the prodigious amount of LBO (Leveraged Buyout) activity - most notably remembered for the KKR (Kohlberg Kravis Roberts) leveraged buyout of RJR Nabisco for $25 billion, a transaction that closed in 1989. Inevitably when referencing this period, aggressive financiers like Michael Milken and Ivan Boesky come up in conversation – both individuals ended up serving relatively short periods of hard jail time. Incidentally, the rise and fall of Drexel Burnham

Lambert's junk bond era was beautifully chronicled in James B. Stewart's *Den of Thieves* and Connie Bruck's *The Predators' Ball.*

Our current real estate crisis can be traced back over a period extending beyond the last 25 years. Ever since long-term treasury interest rates peaked in 1981 around 15% and Federal Reserve Chairman Paul Volcker kicked inflation in the butt, long-term treasury rates have consistently trended downwards to the point now where 10-Year Treasury rates have been yielding consistently at or below the 4% level for the majority of 2008. For a brief period in September 2008, $40 billion in Treasury Bills were sold for a meager 0.05% - rates similar to stuffing money under a mattress. As rates continued to decline over time, professional fixed income money managers and other investors became more and more starved for yield. Unfortunately reality does not mimic English rock band Dire Straits' lyrics where one can get "Money for nothing, chicks for free."

The yield-starved investors had to take on much more risk by investing in the toxic tranches of CDOs (Collateralized Debt Obligations) and other exotic mortgage backed derivative securities. Much, if not most, of the time the investors were taking on risk of which they were unaware. Warren Buffett underscored the ludicrousness of these Residential Mortgage Backed Securities (RMBS) when he talked about a CDO squared product (the packaging of 50 various security slices) which would require the investor to read 750,000 pages of legal documents in order to have a full understanding of the security they owned. My book is hard enough to read as is, just imagine 750,000 pages!

Wall Street and the investment banks were more than happy to package this waste together, for a fat fee of course. As fast as they could shovel this garbage, the yield-starved, gluttonous hedge funds and fixed income money managers gobbled down these real estate securities in their fund troughs. For the bankers, it was like fishing, except no effort was required since the fish were jumping into the boat.

Dumb investors and greedy bankers were not the only actors in this modern day Greek tragedy. Greedy real estate mortgage brokers/lenders, craving speculators, and naïve homebuyers all contributed to this debacle as well. With the regulators asleep at the switch, a perfect storm came together to produce our current disastrous situation. My brother, Troy Slome, a business litigator for Murphy Rosen & Meylan LLP, crystallized the situation in one particular case he handled. To make a long story short, a homebuyer was denied a loan at Countrywide Bank because of inadequate income, therefore the borrower went on to bank #2 where he lied about his undocumented income in order to gain the necessary credit approval. No-doc or low-doc lending was prevalent at the time, but the wrinkle in the story occurred when the borrower went to refinance his loan and he found out that his mortgage broker had forged his signature in order to rake in an extra $500 in pre-payment penalty fees. This true story is just a microcosm of the many shady practices that were going on behind the scenes in this mortgage meltdown.

What these bubbles show me is no matter how much academic research is conducted, the behavioral aspects of greed and fear will always create periods of inefficiency in the marketplace. These periods of inefficiency generate windows of profit opportunity that can be exploited by brainy hedge fund managers like William Ackman of Pershing Square Capital Management. He shorted mortgage security insurer MBI and Ambac and pocketed gobs of cash as the stocks plummeted by more than 90% in less than a 12-month timeframe. On the flip side, identifying these bubbles before they pop can also preserve vast amounts of capital for those investors that do not have the ability or desire to short securities. The Ultra fund I managed, which will be described in more detail later, safeguarded tremendous amounts of capital for our shareholders by identifying the bursting technology bubble earlier than our competitors in the early 2000s.

Efficiency Conclusions

With all these bubbles behind us, what will be the next "bubble" of the 21st century? Perhaps energy and commodities? Emerging markets? Foreign currencies? Ethanol? Britney and Brangelina paparazzi photos?! From the Tulip-mania of the mid-17th century to the recent subprime and mortgage meltdown of 2007-2008, one thing remains clear – history tends to repeat itself, and as a result, greed and fear will remain permanent fixtures of society as long as we homo-sapiens roam this planet.

Throughout this discussion on market efficiency and bubbles, I think my viewpoint is clear. I lean in the camp that the evidence is overwhelmingly in favor that markets go through many periods of inefficiencies (often driven by behavioral factors) that consequently can be exploited for profits. Eventually the markets recognize these imbalances, often in a harsh manner – remember bubbles take much longer to inflate than they take to burst. I think immortalized investor, Benjamin Graham, summed it up best when he said, "In the short-term, the stock market is a voting machine; in the long-term a weighing machine."

Chapter 4: Investment Philosophy

Peachy Concept

Investing is both an art and a science. Focusing too much on either aspect is problematic. Day traders that completely rely on their gut for all their decision making end up getting whipped around at inopportune times, while the straight 'black box' quantitative investors suffer ultimately because any advantage from a purely model-based approach eventually gets competed away by copycat arbitragers. If peaches are on sale at the local grocer for 5 cents/pound, eventually word gets out and the opportunity evaporates…no more 5 cent peaches!

Investing: Mixing Art with Science

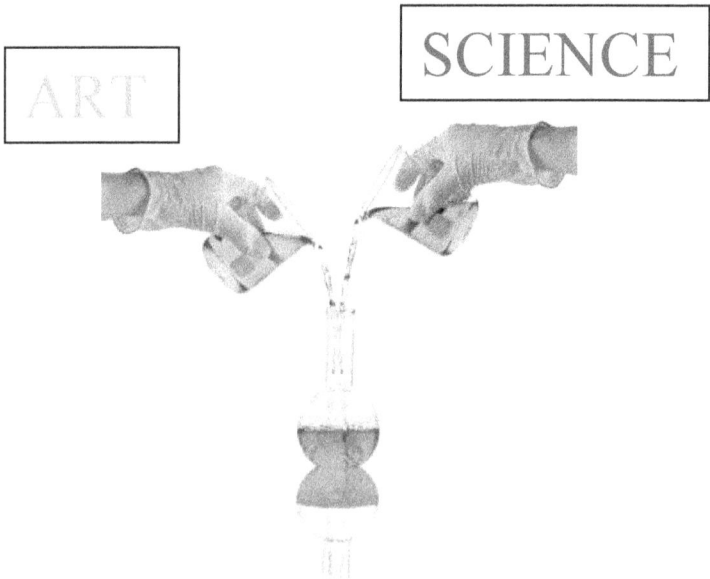

The Science

Instead of peach pricing, many quantitative models focus on a mixture of factors and algorithms using various statistical techniques. Statistical regression involves comparing a 'Dependent Variable' (you can think of an event or outcome) with 'Independent Variables' (things that cause a change in the Dependent Variable), 'Constant Variables', and 'Error Terms'. Typically these quantitative models used to build investment portfolios are designed to predict or explain causal relationships.

Predicting which stocks will go up the most in price is one obvious long strategy that a lot of models try to predict. For example, consider a multi-factor model that takes years of historical data ranging from valuation metrics (i.e. P/E, P/B, EV/EBITDA, dividend yield), return metrics (ROIC, ROE), profitability metrics (gross margins, operating margins, net margins), growth metrics (sales growth, earnings growth, dividend growth), and quality metrics (accrual ratios, debt levels, etc). Once all these various independent variables are crunched through a computing intensive algorithm, a lot of models will spit out an optimal mixture of weightings designed to predict what will create the highest returns in the future.

The number and types of models are virtually endless. By introducing new or different variables that you believe impact stock returns (inflation, management tenure, research & development budget, marketing spending, etc.), the list of input factors is virtually endless. There are multiple types of regression methods including linear regression, polynomial regression, Bayesian regression, logistical regression, and nonparametric regression, not to mention other modeling techniques like Monte Carlo simulation. Monte Carlo simulation is a type of algorithm that repeatedly samples data from a large set of data. Due to the number of repeated random scenarios, the goal is to have a probabilistic view of various outcomes, including the probability of achieving a certain return in the stock market.

Inherent in all these models, there are a whole host of potential issues and drawbacks. My biggest beef with respect to models is that past performance rarely matches future performance; yet inherent in almost every model is the belief that through our understanding of historical relationships of variables we will be able to predict how these variables will impact future returns. Future performance and variable relationships very rarely match the past. However historical performance and relationships may rhyme with the future. The adage that "correlation does not equal causation" is an important credo to follow when reviewing various models.

To honestly rely on these regression outputs one has to rely on a whole host of additional assumptions including the following:

- The sample of data must be representative of the outcomes you are trying to predict.

- The error factor is assumed to be a random variable.

- Regression models assume independent variables are error-free.

- There must not be any collinearity between variables.

- Homoscedasticity exists – constant variances between errors.

Unfortunately these assumptions often do not hold. If you haven't noticed by now, I am not a huge believer in pure quantitative investing or strategies that primarily rely on models for stock selection. Like some other forms of analysis, I view quantitative modeling as a tool and therefore should be treated as such.

The collapse of Long Term Capital Management should be a lesson to everyone. If world renowned Nobel Prize winners, Robert Merton and Myron Scholes, can single-handedly bring the global market to its knees as a result of using inconsistent and unreliable quantitative models, then I feel a lot better about my fundamental-based investment approach. Witnessing economic legends fail is not much different than the feeling one gets from watching a professional golf tournament as a pro shanks a ball into the trees or the water (like most of us hacking weekend-warriors). Fortunately for the pro golfers, their miscues do not negatively impact the global economy by billions or trillions of dollars.

The Art

"It's tough to make predictions, especially about the future..."
-Yogi Berra

Predicting the future is not easy and that is what good stock pickers must do. When it comes to growth stock investing, my philosophy is fairly straight forward. I invest in market leading franchises that can sustain above average growth rates because I believe price follows earnings over the long term. I am in agreement with Peter Lynch when he notes, "People may bet on hourly wiggles of the market, but it's the earnings that waggle the wiggle long term." Therefore the key to success is identifying companies that can maintain exceptional earnings growth. Superior earnings growth will lead to superior price appreciation over the long-term. When Michael Dell asked Peter Lynch about what factors make stocks (including DELL) go up, Mr. Lynch simply replied, "If your earnings are higher in 5 years, your stock will be higher." I concur in spirit – although there will always be exceptions.

Valuation is an art as well. Unfortunately, the market consists of emotional individuals that constantly change their minds on what a company is worth. Eventually the market prods you in the right direction; but over shorter time intervals, proper analysis requires a little wetting the finger and sticking it in the air. Unlike a lot of pure momentum investors, I take valuation very seriously. Overpaying for stocks is a risky strategy that often ends badly. The phenomenon that I notice most often is the tendency for investors to overpay for the hot stocks of the day that are constantly in the newspaper headlines. I'm on the same page with Bill Miller (famed Legg Mason investor extraordinaire) with respect to his views on price efficiency, "If it's in the papers, it's in the price. One needs to anticipate, not react." Usually a news event that makes headlines is already factored into the stock price. More important than short-term valuation metrics is a focus on the long-term earnings growth prospects of a company.

Looking at straight P/E (Price Earnings) can get quite tricky when you are looking at cyclical companies as well. In many cases you want to buy these companies when the current valuation metrics make the stock appear expensive. Since earnings are distorted in periods of weakness during the troughs of economic cycles – the price (numerator) might not come down as quickly as the decline in earnings (denominator), thereby increasing the stock's P/E ratio. "Wait for a recession when the PEs are high, you don't want to buy these when valuations are cheap because they are near peak," noted Peter Lynch. What you really want to concentrate on are "normalized" earnings - a rational level of projected earnings that can be reasonably expected to be achieved in the middle of an economic cycle. The market is always looking forward, not backwards.

When Google went public at $85 per share, the broad Wall Street view was that the IPO price was way overheated. Earnings growth ended up more than quintupling in less than three years and the stock price quintupled as well, showing that focusing on traditional valuation metrics can lead you in the wrong direction. As it turned out, Google was trading at less than nine times 2006 earnings when it went public in 2004. Certainly there are not a bevy of Googles lying around all over the marketplace; however this long-term valuation principal even applies to companies that do not have the same hyper-growth Google experienced in the first few years following its IPO (See Google illustration below).

Valuation is important; however, growth that can be sustained for long periods of time is even more critical. Again I stand in the camp with my buddy Peter when he says, "People concentrate too much on the 'P' (Price), but the 'E' (Earnings) really makes the difference." What appears expensive in the short-run is, in many cases, wildly cheap based on future earnings growth. The lessons learned through legendary trader Jesse Livermore's *Reminiscences of a Stock Operator* provide a similar point regarding valuation and are consistent with Mr. Livermore's comments when he asserted, "Prices are never too high to begin buying or too low to begin selling." Investing in an out of favor growth stock is different from investing in a "value-trap", akin to the attempts of sucking the last drag out of a cigarette butt grabbed from the ground. Peter Lynch adds, "Just because a stock is cheaper than before is no reason to buy it, and just because it's more expensive is no reason to sell."

When it comes to purchasing stocks, I use a different approach. I am much more willing to dip into my wallet to pay extra for a .300 hitter than a .200 hitter on my portfolio team of stocks. I would rather pay a premium for the scarcity value of a good growth stock, than settle for a cheap stock with deteriorating long-term fundamentals.

Market leaders tend to have a competitive advantage, whether in the form of superior research and development, low-cost manufacturing, marketing, and/or other areas in the company that allows the entity to consistently garner more and more market share from its competitors. Quality franchises tend to employ first-class management teams that have a proven track record along with thoughtful, systematic processes in place to maintain their competitive leads. These competitive advantages are what allow companies to produce exceptional earnings growth for extended periods of time, thereby producing exceptional long-term performance.

Too often, investors spend excessive time focusing on price entry and exit points with the false belief that they can precisely time the exact purchase and sales prices. It is better to make a small purchase in a franchise that you love, and add more aggressively on a pullback. Timing the bottom in stock prices is virtually impossible. Or as Bill Miller puts it, "Nobody buys at lows and sells at highs except liars."

Price Follows Earnings
S&P 500 Index (1987-2006)

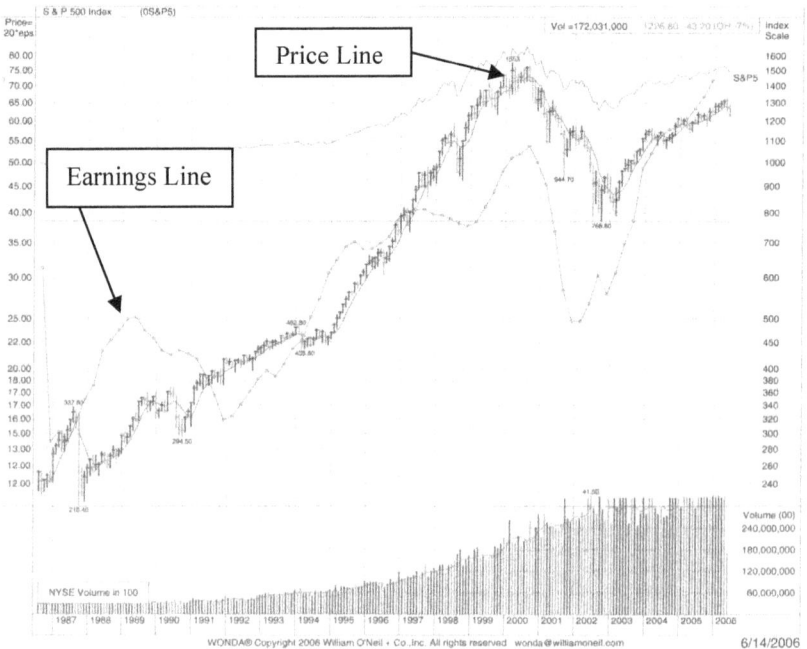

(Chart provided by William O'Neil & Co., Inc.)

A standard method of valuing a fixed income security is discounting future cash flows to the present, thereby arriving at a market price. Conceptually, the discounting mechanism should be no different for equity securities. As mentioned earlier, companies that can sustain above average growth in earnings (and cash flows) consistently into the future will be afforded higher stock prices. Fundamental analysis contributes to the identification of these superior sustained earnings franchises. An additional kicker to sustained high growth rates is realized through multiple expansion (i.e. a higher stock price paid for an earnings stream due to investor confidence). Without patience, the benefits of compounding earnings growth cannot be achieved.

In some instances, relative strength can be a leading indicator of business improvement before the better results show up in a company's financial reports. William O'Neil conducted a study on the Greatest Stock Winners of all-time since the 1950s. His results highlighted the fact that the average relative strength ranking from the beginning of a stock's outperformance ("breakout") was a score of 82.8 (on a scale of 0-100 with 100 being the best performers). Another technical tool to add to one's tool-belt is volume analysis. As William O'Neil has proven throughout his decades of research, supply-demand clues can be acquired and used to help better identify pivot points in emerging trends, whether improving or deteriorating.

"Long Runways of Growth"

The Growth Company Life Cycle

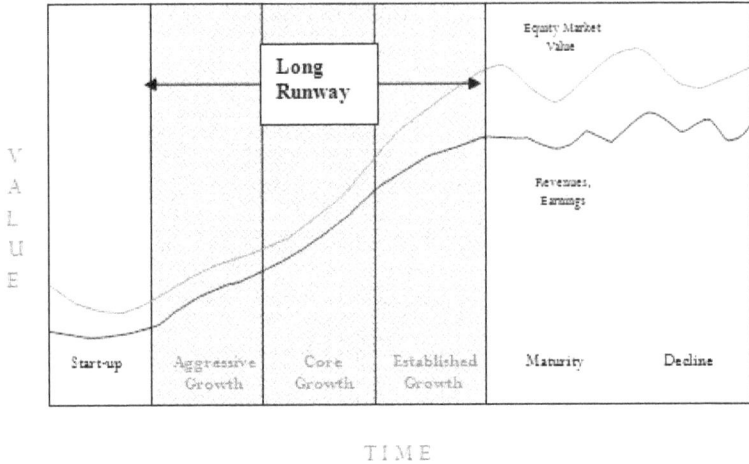

We have reviewed the concept of "Price Follows Earnings" and the extending idea that companies earning above average rates for long periods of time should experience superior price returns. When stock price action diverges dramatically from the trend in earnings growth (e.g. a stock drops 50% in price when earnings growth temporarily drops from 15% to 10%), the resulting price earnings compression can represent an excellent buying opportunity - especially if you believe the growth slowdown is transitory.

Critical in this process of identifying stocks with "long runways" is to single out those companies that are emerging at the earlier stages of their growth cycle. Meticulous fundamental research, using both a Porter's 5 Forces Analysis (1. Bargaining Power of Suppliers; 2. Bargaining Power of Customers; 3. Threat of new Entrants; 4. Threat of Substitute Products; 5. Competitive Rivalry within an Industry) from an industry perspective, coupled with rigorous bottom-up analysis (i.e. financial modeling and forecasting, comprehensive background and document overviews, management interviews, valuation breakdowns, and more) is a broad framework to help identify companies that are early in their growth cycles. Finding a phenomenal investment opportunity with a long runway is easier said than done. "A company does not tell you to buy it, there is always something to worry about. There are always respected investors that say you are wrong. You have to know the story better than they do, and have faith in what you know," expressed Peter Lynch.

As companies reach the 'Mature' phase of their life cycle, earnings growth becomes tougher to achieve and so does stock price appreciation. Warren Buffett's Berkshire Hathaway is anchored with this problem of size and maturity, and Mr. Buffett does not shy away from acknowledging this when referring to the law of large numbers. He straightforwardly says, "Gravity always wins."

When analyzing companies with durable, long runways of earnings growth, I concentrate on those emerging, share-taking companies and dominant market leaders. In other words, companies that are entering new markets with vast potential and companies that are gaining significant share in large markets. "The greatest investment rewards come to those who by good luck or good sense find the occasional company that over the years can grow in sales and profits far more than industry as a whole," said renowned growth authority, Phil Fisher. Finding sustainable growth in niche competitive markets is nearly impossible to discover, and that is why I center my attention on large or emerging sectors of the economy that can support long runways of growth.

Emerging growth trends surround us every day in multiple forms: in technology, we are seeing internet services and applications consumed globally by 1.5 billion people and the explosion of wireless applications permeate through our daily lives; in healthcare, we are witnessing a $4 trillion global healthcare market growing much faster than global economies due to the proliferation of life extending medicines and medical equipment; the alternative energy resource sector promises to introduce tremendous opportunities through aggressive implementation of new and existing energy applications such as wind, solar, nuclear, and bio-fuels; and emerging international markets like Brazil, Russia, India and China stand to experience considerably faster growth as globalization pulls these developing nations into the 21st Century.

Since I am an absolute return investor, I am agnostic to where I find earnings growth. When it comes to the style or security categorization, I am indifferent to how consultants cram managers or stocks into one of the nine convenient Morningstar style boxes. I am merely concerned about how I can maximize upside returns while minimizing downside risk. Styles are constantly moving in and out of favor. The late 1990s was dominated by the Growth style and the early 2000s by the Value style. Mean reversion is a powerful force and as Steven Galbraith, the chief U.S. strategist at Morgan Stanley, smartly points out, "Reversion to the mean is the most powerful force in finance, figuring out the when is the hard part. Still it almost always pays to buy fear and sell greed." Now that we are well into 2008, it appears we have started another cyclical swing back into the Growth camp. Precise timing with respect to trade execution is impossible to predict; but after a strong Growth showing in 2007, it feels like the Growth segment's outperformance will continue once the economic tide turns.

The Value strategy is better suited for investing in companies entering the "mature" phase of their life cycles, while other

Growth strategies generally are better aligned to identifying riskier start-up companies with more growth potential. Mature companies typically serve as fertile ground for those Value managers that stick to their knitting and do not style drift from their stated investment objectives.

In a diversified Growth portfolio, I would own a broad set of Growth stocks across the various segments of the Growth Life Cycle (Aggressive, Core, and Established Growth).

Anticipating and Forecasting Change is a Source of Value-Add

I do not seek to gamble on today's fad stocks, but rather I choose to invest in tomorrow's market winners. Stating it differently, I am constantly pushing to anticipate economic outcomes not seen around the corner, rather than reacting to what I see in the rear-view mirror. I concur with Bill Miller when he stated, "We expect the stocks we buy today to contribute to our performance several years hence. While it's nice if they contribute to this year's performance, this year's performance should be driven by decisions we made in previous years. If we keep doing this, we hope that we will provide adequate returns in the future."

I also believe certain areas of the market are more efficient than others. I argue that the Large Cap Growth market is significantly more efficient than other areas of the market and therefore requires more intensive fundamental forecasting of future trends if an edge over peers will be shaped. I trust that if stock information is broadly exhibited in daily newspaper and magazine headlines, then that information is likely to be discounted into the current stock price. There are over 10,000 Mutual Funds and 10,000 Hedge Funds globally; therefore I believe the vast majority of investors cannot create an edge by reacting faster than the thousands of competing peers that eagerly consume and regurgitate daily news items. Let's not forget to mention the deluge of Wall Street research that floods the investor marketplace. As manager of the $20 billion Ultra Fund, I frequently received more than 400 emails per day, 75 voicemails, 30 pages in faxes, and a small tree's worth of hard-copy analyst reports sent directly to me by snail mail.

For instance, at last check there is an average of 30 analysts each covering Microsoft, Google, and Wal-Mart. Beating the herd at the same game utilized by the masses is a tough chore, so devising alternative strategies is imperative. Superior returns are achieved by independently anticipating events via rigorous homework, not by merely reacting to the headline du jour.

In order to act independently, one must embrace uncertainty. Don Hays, strategist and principal at Hays Advisory Services, was quoted as saying, "NOTHING is certain. Good investors LOVE uncertainty."

Over the previous decades, investment time horizons have been narrowing but academic research shows that investor success has not improved. John Bogle of Vanguard highlighted in 2005 that mutual fund portfolio turnover (a proxy for holding period) has gone from a 17% turnover level in the 1950s (approximately an average 6 year holding period) to 108% in the 2000s (a holding period of less than 1 year. If manager performance is not improving, it is my belief that long term excess returns will only be created by moving away from the herd and taking a longer than average time horizon. My solution: apply a disciplined process that buys fear and sells greed, coupled with a multi-year average portfolio holding period.

When contemplating contrarian investment strategies, the TV show *Seinfeld* comes to mind - specifically, the episode where the character George Costanza realizes that all his instincts are wrong and he decides to do everything the opposite. When George runs into the blonde bombshell, rather than boast about his accomplishments he tells her that he is unemployed and he lives at home with his parents. No worries, George gets the girl. George doesn't stop there because in the same episode he gets his way with New York Yankee owner, George Steinbrenner, by telling him off. There are many ways to skin a cat successfully on Wall Street; however I believe the only true path to long term success is by operating differently than the herd.

Quantifying Conviction, Measuring Upside and Downside Risk

To ensure an objective implementation of my investment philosophy, I have created a system that ranks my targeted universe from top to bottom. The key quantitative factors I focus on include: sales and earnings growth, free cash flow per share growth, adjusted free cash flow growth (adjusted for depreciation and amortization), returns on invested capital (ROIC), relative industry margins/profitability, leverage (debt levels), earnings quality, and valuation (price/free cash flow, price/earnings, enterprise value/EBITDA ratios, others). This impartial process guarantees a more steady approach to investing. It is crucial to look at things rationally and quantitatively rather than dramatically and emotionally.

From a qualitative standpoint, factors such as market share, management quality, pricing power, competitive advantages, barriers to entry, industry growth dynamics, financial transparency/disclosure are among many of the softer factors I consider – think Porter's 5 Forces. Take Amazon.com as an example. This is an innovative technology company veiled under a retailer umbrella that has an e-commerce leadership position. Amazon's software features and functions are unrivaled as compared to peers and have created a huge competitive advantage. The company's financial position (huge free cash flow, low debt levels, and rapid growth) gives it a unique standing in the industry and allows them to deepen their competitive advantages over all types of online/offline retailers. More and more purchases are migrating online, and Amazon is catching the larger shares of these dollars over time.

At its base level, investing is a probabilistic endeavor where the objective of the game is to find situations with odds that favor winning over time. This is where we want to focus our attention.

"I'd bet $1 billion on the flip of a coin if the odds were 3 to 2 in my favor," said Warren Buffett. As investors we must be mindful of the business fundamentals and the expectations (optimistic or pessimistic) already reflected in the asset price. "Stocks do not get undervalued unless somebody is worried about something. The question is not whether there are problems. There are always problems. The question is whether those problems are already fully discounted or not," Bill Miller underscores. Modeling and valuation methodologies are used to create a price target (expected return), which is applied as a barometer against the targeted universe of securities. When rebalancing and reviewing my portfolios, I am constantly reinforcing the principal that my largest positions should be concentrated in the stocks that have the highest expected return and these stocks will be funded with the lowest expected return stocks. The principle in shorting stocks and ranking them accordingly, based on expected returns works just as well in reverse. Again, by quantitatively ranking one's stock, universe investors can limit the creep of unproductive emotions and improve objectivity. Incorporating all these factors will improve your investing probabilities of success.

Investing vs. Gambling

"A professional gambler is not looking for long shots, but for sure money." – Jesse Livermore (legendary trader)

Exhibit 2: Investing and Gambling

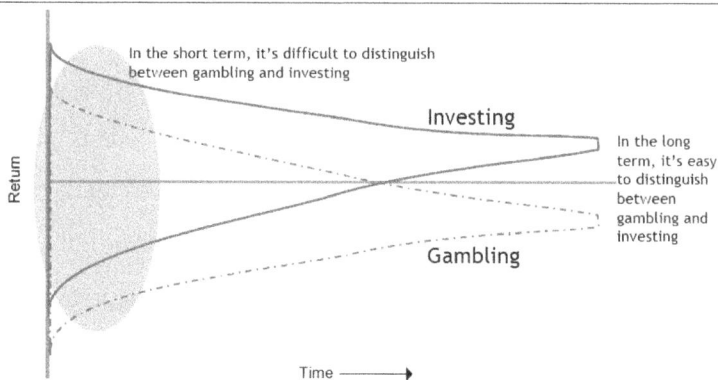

In the short term, it's difficult to distinguish between gambling and investing

Investing

In the long term, it's easy to distinguish between gambling and investing

Return

Gambling

Time

Source: LMFM analysis.

(The probabilistic approach of ranking portfolio securities allows one to rationally allocate capital without constantly reacting to daily volatility and wasteful emotions created from short term market unpredictability.)

Gamblers generally like to move lots of transactions. How many people do you know who travel to Las Vegas, play one hand of

Blackjack and then leave right away? The preponderance of gamblers compromise their "beauty sleep" in exchange for the hope of making a pot of gold. With increased trading, "day-traders" create their set of hoops to jump through – each trade transaction requires that the speculator be right "twice." One has to be right on the initial sell decision and again be right with the subsequent buy decision. For the average investor, the probability of being right twice goes down and hence the degree of difficulty increases. When out on the lake fishing, I believe the strategy of constantly pulling the line out of the water and changing the lure and bait in hopes of catching the "big one" is the mistaken strategy. A better approach is to pick the right bait/lure combination up front, locate the best spot on the lake and then keep your line in the water.

So, what are some of the characteristics of a successful fisherman? In the study below (a mixture of Growth and Value managers), the common characteristic across these market leaders is high concentration (37% in Top 10) and low turnover of 28% (vs. 110% for all equity funds). Gerald Loeb, famed investor and author of *The Battle for Investment Survival,* points out: "The greatest safety lies in putting all your eggs in one basket and watching the basket." A lower portfolio turnover strategy allows investors to benefit from "compounding" - what Einstein called the "Eighth Wonder of the World". (See also Chapter 8: Winning Strategies)

Exhibit 1: Some General Equity Funds that Beat the S&P 500 (1992–2002)

Fund Name	Ten Year Return	Ten Year After Tax Return	Turnover	Assets in Top Ten Holdings
Calamos Growth A	18.7%	15.3%	79%	21.5%
Fidelity New Millennium	17.2	14.5	91	30.3
Legg Mason Value Trust	16.6	15.3	25	51.9
WasatchCore Growth	16.0	13.5	76	46.1
Janus Small Cap Value Institutional	15.8	12.8	39	22.5
Clipper	15.5	12.3	48	51.9
WeitzPartners Value	15.4	13.2	10	50.8
Excelsior Value & Restructuring	15.4	14.7	8	28.1
Weitz Value	14.9	12.9	13	50.1
Longleaf Partners	14.8	12.4	18	57.7
Sequoia	14.8	13.2	8	79.4
Fidelity Low - Priced Stock	14.7	11.6	26	17.1
Smith Barney Aggressive Growth	14.6	13.9	1	53.0
Vanguard Primecap	13.9	12.7	11	35.6
Dodge & Cox Stock	13.8	11.7	13	23.7
Torray	13.5	12.5	23	40.1
T. Rowe Price MidCap Growth	13.5	12.7	36	20.6
GabelliValue A	13.3	9.9	16	39.9
Longleaf Partners SmallCap	13.2	11.5	17	60.0
Heartland Value	13.0	11.2	49	19.3
American Funds Growth Fund of America	12.7	10.2	30	22.7
Federated Kaufmann K	12.5	10.4	65	34.5
Ariel	12.5	9.9	6	36.9
Scudder Dreman High Return Equity A	12.4	10.2	25	52.0
T. Rowe Price Small - Cap Value	12.3	10.6	12	14.9
Liberty Acorn Fund Z	12.3	10.1	13	13.2
Elfun Trusts	12.1	10.0	9	38.9
Franklin Small - Mid Cap Growth	12.1	10.3	47	16.5
PIMCO NFJ Small Cap Value Institutional	12.1	9.9	40	10.2
Dreyfus Appreciation	10.9	10.2	2	41.9
White Oak Growth Stock	10.5	10.4	15	61.5
Average	**13.9%**	**11.9%**	**28%**	**36.9%**
Vanguard 500 Index	9.9 %	9.0 %	7 %	24.1%
Vanguard Total Stock Mkt Idx	9.3	8.5	9	19.4

Source: Morningstar.com.

Valuation Important but Sustained Earnings Critical

The important thing is not what you pay for the stock, so much as being right on the company. As Peter Lynch stated, "If your earnings are higher in five years, chances are that your stock will be higher." In general people tend to concentrate too much on the P (Price) and not enough on the E (Earnings) and that's why I focus on above-average sustainable earnings growth. I do focus on valuation and do not want to overpay for earnings; however, "cheapness" should not be the sole reason for buying a security, nor should "expensiveness" be the main reason for selling. By and large, there is a worthy reason why a stock is trading cheaply or dearly. Intensive modeling of sales, earnings, cash flows, margins, debt and other financial metrics must be employed (see Template below). Valuation sensitivity is much more important for companies living in the mature portion of their growth life cycles.

Long Term Growth in Earnings = Long Term Growth in Stock Price

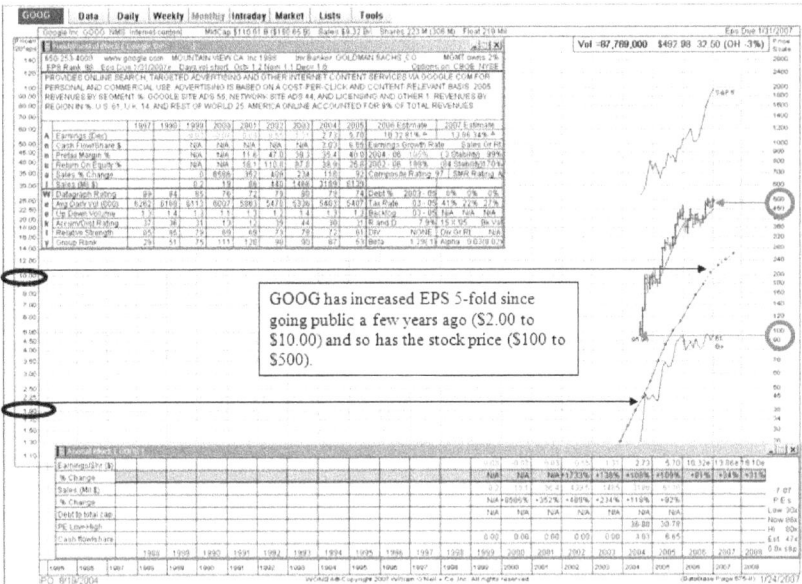

(Upon going public many pundits believed Google to be wildly too expensive and as earnings continued to grow the stock exploded upwards.)

Model & Valuation Template Example:

(The type is small, but this template contains the major building blocks of an effective financial model. Each model is further customized for company and industry specific metrics.)

Active Management is Required to Outperform over the Long Run

It is tough to beat an index if you simply try to mimic the index. Under this strategy, one should expect no more than average returns. Actually, one should expect below average returns once management fees, transactions costs, bid-ask spreads, and trading impact costs are accounted for. Impact costs are the added outlays paid, either in the form of higher prices for consecutive buy trades or lower prices received for consecutive sale trades. The more shares traded consecutively, the larger the damaging impact costs become, thereby hampering performance further.

Portfolio Management

Moreover, I seek to concentrate my portfolio in my best ideas and generally this translates into about 30-40 securities for my hedge fund long positions and 0-20 short ideas. Warren Buffett sees eye-to-eye with Gerald Loeb when Warren states that "I prefer to keep all my eggs in one basket and watch that basket closely." One cannot ignore the benefits of diversification, but academic research shows that the predominant benefits are achieved from a relatively small number of securities as compared to most fund portfolios and stock indexes. In many cases, the largest long-term winners don't start off as the biggest weightings, but due to the compounding of returns, position sizes can explode over time. As Lynch says, "You don't need a lot of good hits every day. All you need is 2-3 good stocks a decade."

My security and sector allocations will vary over time, dependent on where I see the greatest opportunities (expected returns) and in part where we stand in the market cycle. In a perfect world it would be nice to be diversified across all sectors ("diversity helps avoid adversity"); however, in certain instances, my security selection and sector concentration decisions will lead me to avoid sub-sectors or industries altogether. Remember, the main objective is to maximize risk-adjusted, after-tax returns, and if being naked in certain areas of the market helps me achieve that goal, so be it. This is not an original idea - just listen to what successful and prominent growth manager, T. Rowe Price, had to say, "The growth stock theory of investing requires patience, but is less stressful than trading, generally has less risk, and reduces brokerage commissions and income taxes."

Idea Generation

Remember, successful investing is an endeavor that involves the practices of both art and science – too much of either approach is detrimental to your financial health. Quantitative screening is an excellent method in identifying new securities for research along with streamlining the fundamental analysis process. On the qualitative front, I strive to maintain an entrepreneurial culture of idea generation. In addition to quantitative screening metrics, I conduct in-depth fundamental research through continual management team consultations, attend industry analyst meetings, administer field interviews, and travel to conferences/conventions. Not only does this endeavor solidify and challenge the long or short theses of portfolio positions, but this effort also generates valuable new ideas for future possible investments.

Portfolio Maintenance

To ensure the most appropriate risk/reward profile for my portfolios, I set price targets and ranges for each security in the portfolio. These targets/ranges are considered in conjunction with the quantitative metrics uncovered in the new ideas screening process. Sometimes new ideas come from the mathematical side of research (i.e. screens), while at other times ideas come straight from a conversation, article, or visit to the local mall. The artistic aspects of investing cannot be underestimated. A standardized, detailed multi-year model is also developed for each company, outlining future revenue, earnings, and cash flow growth (among other factors), not to mention key corporate statistics and balance sheet figures. As mentioned earlier, under this framework, I believe it is crucial to evaluate things rationally and quantitatively, rather than dramatically and emotionally.

Investment Philosophy Overview

For any philosophy to endure, a consistent core set of beliefs needs to be followed. My core beliefs revolve around earnings growth, valuation, and competitive advantage. Most flourishing philosophies include some combination of these, although different styles (Growth vs. Value) will emphasize each factor to a different extent. Value managers concentrate less on earnings growth and more on valuation.

Over time my investment philosophy has evolved into a disciplined 'growth' strategy, borrowing winning ideas from 'growth' investment giants like Peter Lynch, Phil Fisher, William O'Neil, Ron Baron, and John Calamos to name a few. I am not shy to borrow the ideas from 'value' legends like Warren Buffett either. I apply many of his fundamentally oriented concepts that certainly fit stocks that pass through my "strike zone." Let's not forget that Buffett owned some tremendous 'growth' stocks in the 70s and 80s, Coca Cola, Gillette, American Express, Wells Fargo and others that he still owns today – P&G merged with Gillette. He makes clear, "A high ratio of price to book value, a high price-earnings ratio, and a low dividend yield - are in no way inconsistent with a 'value' purchase." In other words, he is willing to pay up for "Growth" stocks.

Regardless of the influences, my philosophy boils down to a focus on market leading franchises that can sustain above average growth rates because of the strong belief that price follows earnings over the long-term. Embedded in my philosophy is the belief that valuation, long-term compounding, and low costs (fees/taxes) contribute to outperformance.

As mentioned earlier, investing is a mixture of art and science. Too much of either component will be hazardous to your investing health. Whatever philosophy one follows, I firmly believe a consistent commitment to philosophical core beliefs is required to succeed. Wavering and waffling is bound to lead to failure.

Chapter 5: Hedge Funds

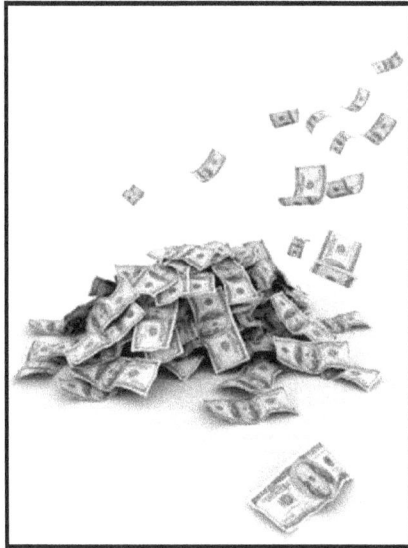

Are those Franklins falling from the sky as a result of hefty hedge fund returns? Or is there a large pile of hedge fund fees falling out of investors' pockets? We will explore these questions and more in this chapter.

What is a Hedge Fund?

People treat the subject with such mystery. From a 10,000 foot level, a hedge fund is not much more than a loosely regulated mutual fund that charges a lot more in fees. Less regulated means hedge fund managers have the flexibility to implement a broader set of secretive strategies, including selling stocks short (profiting from security price declines) and using heavier amounts of leverage (use of debt to buy more assets). My cynicism of hedge funds should probably be questioned, and some may even call hypocritical, since I myself manage a hedge fund. My main motivation in managing a hedge fund is based on the investment freedom that this structure affords me. Because the strategies used by hedge funds are so diverse, and the levels of risk vary considerably from fund to fund, it is critical for investors to investigate and understand the manager's investment strategies and risk control processes before investing.

Industry Statistics

As the chart below highlights, the Hennessee Group LLC, an adviser to hedge fund investors, estimates that the hedge fund industry assets increased dramatically by $462 billion in 2007 alone to $1.997 trillion in assets under management (+30% year-over-year). The slope of the trend is a steep upward trend to the right but nothing lasts forever. However, before this trend ends I hope the growth in my hedge fund can significantly contribute to this trend! The bear market of 2008, coupled with the credit crisis, are bound to negatively impact the slope of this industry chart as fund managers are forced to deleverage and cut back positions.

Hedge Fund Industry Assets (in Billions)
Source: Hennessee Group LLC

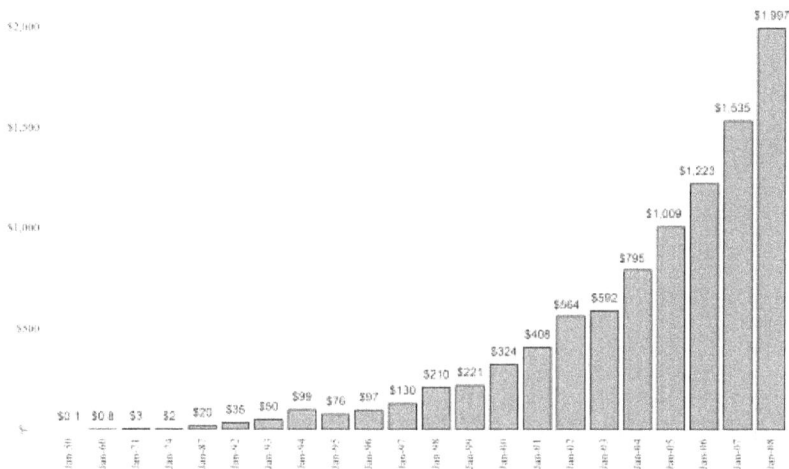

Results from the Hennessee Group's data indicated that the hedge fund industry experienced net inflows of $278 billion (+18%) in 2007. The other $184 billion (+12%) came as a result of positive performance. These figures become even larger if the analysis included assets invested in fund of hedge funds. As hedge fund assets grow, the hedge funds are becoming a larger and larger percentage of daily trading volume – a study in 2003 showed that hedge funds accounted for approximately 25% of average daily trading volume despite their assets only accounting for about 10%

of the market's total assets. This trading volume phenomenon is possible because of the active trading nature of many hedge funds.

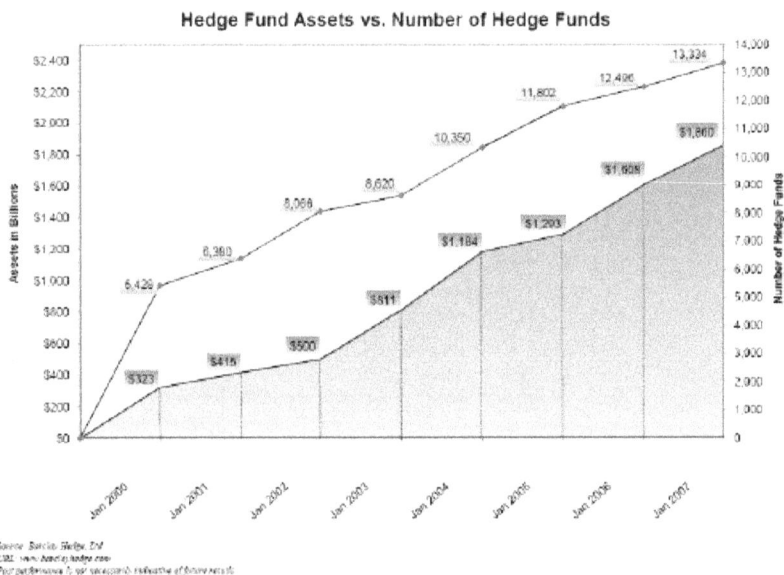

This snapshot from Barclay's provides a perspective on the growth in the number of hedge funds as well.

The Big Bang: Explanations of the Hedge Fund Phenomenon

The data on hedge fund performance is mixed and, in many cases, lacks transparency or the track records necessary to draw meaningful conclusions. If performance is not so remarkable, then why are we seeing explosive growth in the number of hedge funds and asset inflows?

I) The Brain Drain

There is no question Wall Street is suffering a brain drain as talented professionals leave mutual fund companies and high-paying jobs on Wall Street to pursue greener pastures. A lot of green has and continues to be made from lofty hedge fund fees. Institutional investors and pension funds have taken notice, and they have followed the talent by shaking dollars at them. People may question the greedy motives of some hedge fund managers, but the famous bank robber, Willie Sutton, said it best when asked why he robbed banks, "because that's where the money is." Based on their actions, hedge fund managers feel the same way.

II) Return Starved Investors – 25 Year Collapse in Rates

The benchmark long-term interest rates of the early 1980s peaked at around 15% before Paul Volcker, former Chairman of the Federal Reserve, choked off inflation by limiting the growth of the money supply. Through Volcker's courageous efforts, the United States kick started a multi-decade period of declining interest rates where double-digit inflation became a thing of the past. Declining interest rates had a profound influence on the investment climate for businesses to buy new capital equipment and led to tremendous gains in productivity and GDP advancement.

On the flip side however, as we reached the early 2000s with interest rates at 40+ year lows, pensions and institutional investors were starved for more yield and return. The 76 million Baby Boomers were starting into retirement and legacy corporations with gargantuan pension liabilities needed to look for greater returns to meet their obligations. How do we get higher returns? Well, we need to take on more risk. How does one take on more risk? Hmm, hedge funds should to the trick. Voila, and there you have it.

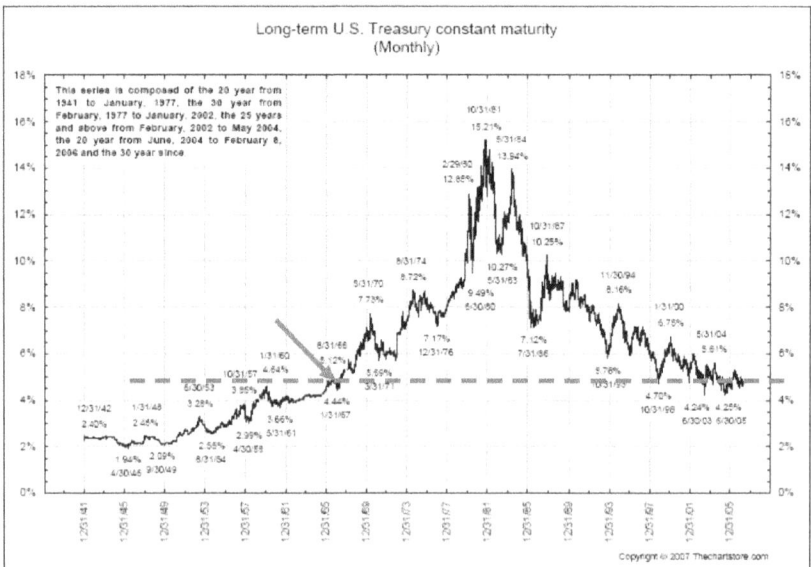

Long-term U.S. Treasury constant maturity (Monthly)

III) Bubble-icious. The Ability to Short a Declining Market
Bill Miller's comment on behavioral finance expert Amos Tversky's research on *losses*: "Loss is painful, on average twice as painful as gain is pleasurable in matters financial.

That is, people on average need about a 2 to 1 payoff on an even odds bet to take the bet. But even a modest advantage yields big gains over time, which is why casinos make so much money."

As the "bubble" began to burst after the peak in March 2000, investors developed a very weak appetite for losses as behavioral finance research intensely documents. The drop was so precipitous that the relative gains by short positioned hedge funds created excess demand. The hedge fund train has been gaining steam ever since. Investors must keep in mind that various styles and products come in and out of style over various cycles.

Hedge Fund Fees

Most of my skepticism relating to hedge funds revolves around what are typically high fee structures. Or, in other words, one must answer whether the high fees hedge funds earn are justified given the returns generated. Academic studies show that the answer is 'NO' in most cases – the investment returns earned by hedge fund managers overall do not adequately compensate hedge fund investors for the hefty fees paid. Typically the standard hedge fund fee structure is quoted as "2 and 20", meaning every year the hedge fund manager gets paid 2% of the NAV (Net Asset Value) along with 20% of profits – sometimes the profits are measured relative to a minimal hurdle rate. Therefore, the gravy train of loaded fees does not kick in until the minimum hurdle rate is exceeded.

In many cases a "high water" mark of performance is created, meaning that subsequent returns earned below the high water mark will not earn an incentive fee. For example, assume that a hedge fund starts the year at $100 million in assets and grows to $130 million in assets by year-end (with no new investment additions or withdrawals). Well, after year one, the manager would have earned $6 million in performance fees (20% X [$130 million - $100 million]) with approximately another $2.3 million from annual investment management fees (approximation of 2% earned on the average of the beginning and ending asset values ($100 million & $130 million), withdrawn typically on a quarterly basis. As of October 2008, the Slome Sidoxia Fund still did not charge a Performance Fee like many hedge funds charge.

With respect to the high water mark fee scheme, what happens in many instances is that once a particular hedge fund falls significantly below the water mark, they just give up and throw in the towel. Rather than patiently wait to grow assets above the high water mark level, the impatient managers would rather close the hedge fund and reopen again with a clean slate under a new name. That way, the new hedge fund can charge high fresh fees again without having to wait a long period of time to crawl above the high water mark.

The Big Get Bigger

As a larger portion of the trillions managed by pensions migrates over to the hedge fund arena in hopes of increasing their returns, these large sophisticated pension investors are demanding more from their hedge funds. Some of these demands come in the form of beefed-up back office support and technology system requirements. Augmented transparency and related reporting capabilities is another area in which pensions are demanding more hand-holding. All of these forces are leading to more assets being funneled into the larger hedge funds. An article written in mid-2007 by Morgan Stanley's prime-brokerage unit, which caters to hedge funds, claimed the 100-largest hedge funds controlled about 70% of the money in the hedge-fund world (up from less than 50% at the end of 2003). Additionally, the 300 hedge funds with $1 billion or more at the time controlled about 85% of all the money in the business.

Hedge Fund Shell-Game and Fund Attrition

Hedge fund attrition has been measured by some to be as high as 20%. A study done by Burton Malkiel, esteemed professor from Princeton, determined from a pool of 604 hedge funds that reported data in 1996, less than 25 percent (or 124 funds) were still around in 2004.

Why such a large attrition rate as compared to traditional mutual fund managers? Well, as I spelled out earlier, the compensation structure for hedge fund managers is pretty darn compelling. If you are in the batter's box and get paid $100,000 for every home run you hit and $1,000 for every single you hit, wouldn't you be swinging for the fences every pitch? And that is what many hedge fund managers do. They strike out and lose too much because of their overly-aggressive strategies. By using excessive leverage to amplify swings in returns, more hedge fund managers suffer financial ruin and are forced to close shop.

Let us assume two scenarios with a common goal of earning a 100% return. If the goal is reached, the fund manager will receive $1 million. Also suppose the only stock we can invest in is Google (GOOG). If Google is trading at $500 today, which of the following strategies would you implement if you were a hedge fund manager trying to earn that $1 million bonus?

- **Strategy A)** Invest $50 and borrow $450 in order to buy 1 GOOG share for $500. If the GOOG share price goes from $500 to $550, the manager just made a $50 return on the initial investment of $50, thereby earning a 100% return and securing the $1 million bonus.

- **Strategy B)** Invest $500 to buy 1 GOOG share for $500. If the GOOG share rises to $1,000, then the manager will have earned 100% and merited the $1 million bonus.

Which strategy sounds easier? Strategy A, where the stock needs to rise $50 to earn the $1 million bonus? Or Strategy B, where the stock needs to rise $500 to earn the $1 million bonus? Well, lo and behold, most hedge fund managers choose 'Strategy A' all day.

Where does the thought process go wrong? Well as great as Strategy A sounds, if GOOG dips from $500 to $450 (-10%), then 100% of the initial investment is lost and you can say "bye-bye" to **Strategy 'A' Capital Management, LLC**. No problem, because that hedge fund can just raise another $50, lease a building across the street and start all over again under a new name…**Strategy 'a' Capital Management, LLC** (I call this the 'Shell Game' – lots of movement to conceal underlying dynamics). I think you get the picture. There are plenty of opportunities to make money in hedge funds, but investors should be wary about the use of excess leverage to swing for the fences.

Bill Gross, renowned bond manager, noted that a *Grants Interest Rate Observer* issue in 2004 asserted nearly three quarters of hedge funds use leverage. The hedge funds on average hold a ratio of 3:1 for assets relative to capital – meaning the managers borrow $2 for every $1 they invest of their own money. Believe it or not, according to this data, banks have an even higher leverage ratio of 10:1 (Assets to Capital) on average.

Recent examples that drive home this point occurred earlier in 2008 when a London hedge fund called Peloton gained 87% in 2007 and was named Credit Hedge Fund of the Year in January 2008. Its long positions in AAA mortgage paper should have continued to hold up better than its subprime shorts. But the AAAs declined this year, and they had bought enough on leverage to make the fund melt down in February. Oh, how things can shift so quickly. Bear Stearns and Lehman Brothers were slightly different animals, but the same principles apply.

If we move back just a few years to 2006, Amaranth Advisors gambled on natural gas prices staying high, and when gas values went against them, the firm ended up slashing the value of its two hedge funds by over 50% in a month.

And who can forget the infamous collapse of Long Term Capital Management (LTCM) in 1998. At the beginning of 1998, shortly before its collapse, Long Term Capital Management had borrowed over $26 for each $1 invested. At the beginning of

September 1998, John Meriwether, the founder, disclosed the fund's gargantuan losses and limited client withdrawals. To give you a flavor for the extent of the trouncing, LTCM lost $500 million in a single day on August 21, 1998. Mr. Meriwether's explanation for the company's subsequent meltdown was direct and to the point: "The Fund added to its positions in anticipation of convergence, yet . . . the trades diverged dramatically." A consortium of 14 Wall Street banks ended up bailing out LTCM for $3.6 billion.

The Silver Lining

For all these horror stories, there certainly are stories of success. Jimmy Rogers, famed hedge manager, now frequently in the press for his bullish stance on commodities and China, first gained notoriety by co-founding the hugely successful Quantum Fund with George Soros (another historical hedge fund manager) in 1970. The Quantum Fund used vast amounts of leverage to achieve a return exceeding 4,000% over the remainder of the decade, despite a tough stock-market environment.

Other examples of well-known hedge fund managers (past and present) that have succeeded wildly include Steven Cohen (SAC Capital Partners); Julian Robertson (Tiger Fund); Michael Steinhardt (founder of Steinhardt Partners); Paul Tudor Jones

(Tudor Group); Ken Griffin (Citadel Investment Group); and Stanley Druckenmiller (Duquesne Capital) among others. Hedge funds are not all evil, and if properly researched can provide diversification benefits to an investment portfolio as an alternative asset class.

Do Your Homework

In this chapter we have covered a broad range of complex hedge fund issues, ranging from fee structures and strategies to risk profiles and transparency. Based on the information provided, I hope awareness has been raised. So if you're thinking about using a hedge fund to bolster your portfolio returns, make sure you perform your due diligence and invest with somebody you trust. Hedge funds are generally overpriced and, in some cases, involve a lot more risk of which the investor is unaware. If you do not understand what you are investing in or the level of risk assumed is unclear, then you are better off investing elsewhere. The legal documents and subscription materials for my Sidoxia Hedge Fund go out of the way to clearly define my strategy along with the range of leverage (risk) I am allowed to assume. For example, investing in a futures strategy uses drastically more leverage than my fund. When investing in hedge funds, make sure you do your homework.

Chapter 6: Managing Billions –
Riding the Bull

"Hey Bruce, are the traders working on that 10 million share order ticket?" I inquired. Bruce responded, "Yep, they've only traded 500,000 shares and we're over 20% of the volume today." Disappointed, I reacted with a deep sigh and then exclaimed, "This sucker is only trading by appointment - this position is gonna take us a month to complete!" This was an ordinary exchange between me and the other portfolio manager, except perhaps for word choice that may have substituted a different word for "sucker".

Because of our size, around $20 billion in assets when I was promoted to portfolio manager on the flagship fund in 2002, our fund was like a large supertanker competing against smaller, more agile speed boats. A trade that might take a $50 million fund nano-seconds to complete could take my fund days, weeks, or even months to complete, depending on the liquidity. On certain occasions we owned such large percentages of companies that we were required to comply with additional regulatory filing procedures because of our sizeable ownership. In other words, we were the elephant in the room that could not hide and were forced to show our hand to all our competitors. Large investors like Warren Buffett are anchored by these requirements as well.

Despite our size, we had a tremendous multi-year run that effectively landed us in a top 25% ranking relative to our peer group (Large Cap Growth funds) on a one, three, five, and ten year basis at the beginning of 2005. I was young and hungry, and my contributions allowed me to climb the ladder until I was co-managing one of the 10 largest LC Growth funds in the country.

INVESTOR'S BUSINESS DAILY

VOL. 21, NO. 63   WWW.INVESTORS.COM   FRIDAY, JULY 9, 2004 $1.21

MUTUAL FUND PROFILE

Ultra Finds Fast Growth In All Cap Sizes

It's Tuned In To Trends

American Century fund is big cap, but is flexible in search for 'next eBay'

BY PAUL KATZEFF
INVESTOR'S BUSINESS DAILY

Like a bloodhound sniffing for clues, American Century Ultra Fund tries to follow trends to find winning stocks.

There's the trend toward more use of broadband access to the Internet. Another trend involves aging baby boomers. Job insecurity pushing people to improve job skills is a third trend.

Overall, the fund's nose hasn't let down shareholders recently.

The $23.5 billion Ultra's TWCUX 1.74% Q2 gain was fourth best among the 25 largest funds tracked by Lipper Inc.

For the year going into Thursday, its 3.04% return of 1.83 percentage points ahead of the S&P 500 and 3.45 points better than its large-cap growth peers tracked by Morningstar.

It has a three-year return of -1.27% vs. -0.49% for the S&P 500 and -4.14% for its peers.

Among the fund's winners this year, eBay EBAY is up about 30%. Web auctioneer is helped by people moving to broadband service.

"People spend more time and money online when they have broadband access," said co-manager Wade Slome.

Zimmer Holdings ZMH is up 26% this year. The firm makes medical devices like artificial joints.

"A company like this benefits from baby boomers who want to be more active in their later years," Slome said. "This firm comes up with materials that increase durability of artificial (implant) devices. And they contribute to surgical procedures that lead to smaller surgical incisions, less pain and speedier recoveries."

Apollo Group APOL is up some 30%. For-profit schools soared during the recession. Adults enrolled to beef up job skills. Despite an improved economy, the schools remain popular.

"Headlines about outsourcing and a jobless recovery keep pushing people to invest in themselves," Slome said. "Apollo differentiated itself from competitors by marrying online courses with classrooms."

The Next eBay

The firm is active in only 32 states. "That leaves them plenty of room for expansion," Slome said. Also, Apollo has classrooms in only some cities in the states it has penetrated, leaving opportunities for growth.

The entire sector pulled back recently on news about regulatory probes into accounting improprieties at some Apollo competitors. The fund looks for firms with earnings improvement and above-average growth.

To find that, it sometimes buys smaller caps, which often grow faster than big caps. "We look for the next Amgen AMGN, eBay and Star-

American Century Ultra		
▪ Managers (yrs.):		
James Stowers III (23), Bruce Wimberly (8), Gerard Sullivan (3), Wade Slome (2)		
▪ Assets: $23.5 bil		
▪ Symbol: TWCUX		
▪ Expenses: 1.00%		
▪ Ph.: (800) 345-2021		

Returns

2003:		25.80%
YTD:		3.04%
3-yr. avg.:		-1.27%
5-yr. avg.:		-3.37%

Wade Slome
Top-rated holdings

	EPS Rating	RS Rating	Acc/Dist Rating
Starbucks	98	90	B+
Whole Foods Market	95	93	A+
Zimmer Holdings	96	91	B-

bucks SBUX," Slome said.

Mid and small caps accounted for 24% of the large-cap fund's money as of May 31. They had been only 17% 12 months earlier.

Added to the portfolio starting in January, small-cap JetBlue Airways' JBLU stock gained 16% in Q2. Mid-cap Chicago Mercantile Exchange Holdings CME rose 49% in Q2 and is up 95% for the year.

The operator of the futures and options market was 0.4% of the fund as of April 30, but is not in the S&P 500, mid-cap 400 or small-cap 600.

"If you find names like that, you differentiate yourself from indexes and peers," Slome said. "The firm benefits from globalization of financial markets. It is (replacing human traders) with an electronic platform. That improves liquidity and

improves profits."

Still, the fund has top-performing large caps.

Tyco International TYC, $64 billion in size, is up 21% this year. Many investors are distracted by controversy surrounding the stock, but that is largely related to previous management, Slome says.

"The new CEO, Ed Breen, came from Motorola MOT and cleaned house," Slome said. "He replaced the whole board and reset corporate governance procedures. Old management got growth by acquisitions. Breen focused on improving productive businesses and assets and got bond-rating increases."

Heavenly Hogs

Harley-Davidson HDI, $18 billion in size, is up 29%.

"They're benefiting from baby-boomer demographics," Slome said. "They make an affordable luxury that targets higher-end consumers. They've expanded their product line. And they're expanding into women demographics."

The fund can be volatile, as lagging performance in 2000 and '03 showed. But it can shine in bull markets.

Topping the S&P 500 should be harder this year vs. last year.

"This year's market is flat," he said. "We won't get huge sector outperformance." That will deprive Ultra bloodhounds of easy clues pointing to winning stocks. "We'll have to work hard to find stocks with the earnings gains we want."

(Ultra's prominence was rising, as was mine)

24 Hours in the Life of a $20 Billion Fund Manager

This schedule changes from day to day and week to week, but these events are representative of my daily responsibilities as portfolio manager of the $20 billion Ultra fund.

5:30 a.m. – 5:45 a.m.	Alarm goes off. Take dog outside for toilet pit stop.
5:45 a.m. – 6:00 a.m.	Shower, shave, and brush my fangs. Grab suitcases.
6:00 a.m. – 6:15 a.m.	Watch and race through CNBC & Bloomberg headlines on my TIVO digital video recorder. Take breakfast on the go (banana and oatmeal packets).
6:15 a.m. – 6:45 a.m.	Commute to work while going through 30 of my 75 daily voice mails.
6:45 a.m. – 6:50 a.m.	Hike 16 flights of stairs as part of my Mt. Whitney hiking training.

Reach top floor where my office resides.

6:50 a.m. – 7:45 a.m.   Chew through my first 100 e-mails and another 30-40 voicemails before the market opens, and read through portfolio holding news items on my Bridge System.

7:45 a.m. – 8:45 a.m.   Meet with other PM to discuss any potential fires or trading idea gems.

8:45 a.m. – 10:00 a.m.   Team meeting with analysts to review portfolio and new stock-idea research. Discuss weekly trading strategies opportunities.

10:00 a.m. – 10:15 a.m.   Meet with traders to discuss trading guidelines and strategies for new and previously outstanding trades.

10:15 a.m. – 11:30 a.m.   Conference call with Google (GOOG) co-founder Sergey Brin to discuss reasons behind secondary offering along with China strategy, monetization opportunities, and business seasonality.

11:30 a.m. – 12:00 p.m.   Lunch at desk, watching CNBC over the internet and reading the Wall Street Journal online.

12:00 p.m. – 1:30 p.m.   Wal-Mart (WMT) CEO Lee Scott in our boardroom. Discuss Eduardo Castro-Wright, the new CEO of Wal-Mart Stores USA. Question domestic and international Supercenter rollout and viability of smaller store concept. Also probe management regarding supply chain initiatives and ability to take down inventory to free up capital for other investments.

1:30 p.m. – 2:30 p.m.	Listen to Chicago Mercantile Exchange (CME) quarterly earnings conference call.
2:30 p.m. – 3:00 p.m.	Finish updating my CME model inputs and projections. Go over margin and revenue forecasts with lead analyst on our team.
3:00 p.m. – 3:15 p.m.	Call Goldman Sachs to discuss my one-on-one private management meeting schedule at the Las Vegas Internet Conference next week (Bellagio).
3:15 p.m. – 4:00 p.m.	Car service picks me up to take me to the airport at the American Century private hangar.
4:00 p.m. – 7:30 p.m.	Take private jet while chatting with George Brett, who will also speak to our top clients in New York City at the Waldorf-Astoria. We talk about the infamous pine-tar incident, his relationship with NY Yankee Goose Gossage and

	his hemorrhoids issues that flared up in the 1980 World Series.
7:30 p.m. – 8:00 p.m.	Call wife and kids to say goodnight and blow some kisses over the phone.
8:00 p.m. – 9:30 p.m.	Order in room service as I prepare for speaking event to 250 fund wholesalers the following day.
9:30 p.m. – 11:00 p.m.	Connect laptop and check fund's daily performance and review any news items that may significantly impact trades tomorrow. Execute a mass email deletion, and respond to any important emails – including background information to a Dow Jones writer for a news article on fund.
11:00 p.m. – 11:01 p.m.	Head hits pillow, and I'm out in an instant.
5:30 a.m. to…….	Do it all over again!

Post-Diploma

Coming out of Cornell as a newly minted MBA, I certainly was not targeting Kansas City as my top geographic prospect. But the opportunity to work on a large multi-billion dollar fund, and come on as a generalist analyst practicing rigorous fundamental research across a broad set of industries was an offer I simply could not refuse. Sure, I had other opportunities to work back in my California stomping grounds (among other regions), but in addition to the position, the charm and appeal of the management culture at American Century was an undeniably attractive attribute.

The co-managers of the fund at the time, Bruce Wimberly and John Sykora, were bright, motivated individuals that would help kick start my professional career as well. James "Jimmy" Stowers III, the son of renowned billionaire-philanthropist and founder, James E. Stowers Jr., also acted as a consultant on the fund and sat in on weekly portfolio review meetings. Jimmy had the fortune to help spearhead the fund in glory during the miraculous year of 1991 when Ultra earned a return of 101%.

My unique experience at American Century Investments will always be one I cherish and have fond memories of, but like other firms in the industry, it suffered its fair share of growing pains. Within a period of 16 months (concentrated in 2006-

2007), the company experienced a rash of departures that included President/CEO, Bill Lyons; Chief Financial Officer, Bob Jackson; Chief Investment Officer, Mark Mallon; and Chief Investment Officer (Mid-Cap/Small-Cap Growth), Harold Bradley. Additionally, high profile portfolio manager departures by Bruce Wimberly, John Sykora, Matthew Hudson, and David Rose (among others) coincided with the executive departures, all while Chairman James "Jimmy" Stowers III observed these events from his transatlantic home in London, England. Over the years there were many management decisions I agreed with; however, there were also decisions I disagreed with - including how the fund should be managed. But as my mother taught me from a young age, if you don't have anything good to say, then say nothing at all.

Having said all that, American Century is a great institution founded by the previously mentioned philanthropist, James E. Stowers, Jr. – a man with a pure and generous heart. Jim, along with the help of his wife, Virginia (both cancer survivors), donated more than $1 billion of American Century stock to start the Stowers Institute for Medical Research in 2001, designed to help discover cures for dreaded diseases, including cancer. American Century is deserving of its Fortune Magazine's 'Top 100 Best Companies to Work For' recognition and will be around for years to come.

The Ride Begins

Starting at American Century in 1998 was a strange time. The Asian currency crisis had firmly taken hold, leading to the default of Russian debt, and ultimately, to the collapse of legendary hedge fund, Long Term Capital Management. Believe it or not, crude oil collapsed to $11 per barrel in 1998 (a far cry from the $146 per barrel reached in July 2008), Henry Blodget set his infamous $400 price target for Amazon (which was temporarily surpassed before ensuing stock splits), and Seinfeld's historic comedic run came to a close. What a year!

Eventually I settled in as an analyst covering everything from the retail and energy sectors to financials and some healthcare stocks. My efforts were becoming noticed, but given the inflating technology bubble, it was no surprise much of the portfolio discussions, activity and debate revolved around the technology sector. In fact, at the peak of the market in 2000, the technology sector accounted for more than 50% of the Russell 1000 Growth Index, a key benchmark that Ultra monitored and against which was compensated.

Concentrated technology positions that helped the fund in 1998 and 1999, such as AOL Time Warner (AOL), Qualcomm (QCOM), and Gemstar (GMST) hurt the fund in 2000. It was not uncommon to have multiple 10% weightings in the portfolio. Ultra's technology weighting peaked at 44% in 1999, near the point where total assets topped out at around $43 billion.

The door opened up for me in 2001, when an outside-hired senior analyst (who put a $1 trillion market value forecast on AOL!) decided to resign and take a position in Chicago. I was immediately thrust into the highest profile analyst position in the company, covering the most important sector, technology. My bearish views on technology, due to the massive amounts of excess capacity built in as a result of Y2K and excess B2B/B2C/New Economy infrastructure spending, had an immediate positive impact to the fund. Our 44% position in technology eventually reached a nadir of 9% in 2002. This preserved massive amounts of capital for Ultra shareholders and resulted in the fund being recognized in the top 25% results in both 2001 and 2002. The fund's prominence was rising, and so was mine.

I was promoted to portfolio manager of the Select Fund in July 2002 for a short stint where I also achieved top quartile status on that fund. Towards the end of 2002, senior management pulled me aside and made it clear my contributions would be more effectively used on the larger Ultra flagship fund. I accepted the challenge and began the journey that led us to a top 25% ranking relative to our competitors across a broad range of time periods (one, three, five, and ten years) at the beginning of 2005.

There, I had done it. I had successfully managed a $20,000,000,000 fund by the age of 32!

AMERICAN CENTURY ULTRA FUND

to individual companies. We look for an improving, accelerating growth trend and one that we believe is sustainable. In addition to poring over the numbers, we travel frequently to speak directly with company executives. Our objective is to find growing market leaders that will benefit from long-term, sustainable trends and add them to our portfolio.

Currently, technology and health care are our two largest sector weightings in the portfolio. For many years now, technology and health care have been growing percentages of gross domestic product. Among tech subsectors, we like a handful of Internet companies now. We are just at the start of a long-term, sustainable growth trend in Internet usage. Look at online retail sales, for example. They are growing very, very rapidly while gaining share from the traditional bricks-and-mortar companies. And consider online air travel and hotel bookings: the level has exceeded many forecasts. Also, so far, only about 28% of American households have signed on for broad-band [high-speed Internet access], so there

American Century Ultra Fund

| AVERAGE ANNUAL TOTAL RETURNS AS OF 6/30/04 | | | | | | |
Fund (Inception date)	Symbol	1YR	5YR	10YR	Since Inception
American (11/02/81) Century Ultra	TWCUX	00.0%	0.00%	0.00%	0.00%
S&P 500 (00/00/00)	XXXX	00.0%	0.00%	0.00%	0.00%

For more recent performance information, call Schwab at 877-566-0120. For more complete information about the American Century Ultra Fund, including investment objectives, risks, fees, and expenses, obtain a prospectus from Charles Schwab. Please read the prospectus carefully before investing.

Performance data represents past performance and is no guarantee of future results. Current results may be lower or higher. The share price and investment return of an investment in the American Century Ultra Fund will fluctuate so that, when redeemed, shares may be worth more or less than their original cost. Visit Schwab.com for more recent performance information.

The S&P 500 is an index of 500 widely traded stocks. It is not an investment product available for purchase. (xxx-xxxx)

is room for accelerating growth. Broad-band customers spend more time—and more money—on the Web. Amazon.com (AMZN) is a big fish in a big pond that is getting even bigger. We also own InterActiveCorp (IACI), which owns an assortment of Internet companies, including Expedia and Ticketmaster. In health care, Teva Pharmaceutical Industries (TEVA) is the world's largest manufacturer of generic drugs and we believe it will benefit from efforts to hold down rising health-care costs.

On Investing: American Century Ultra enjoys a four-star rating from Morningstar and handily beat most of its peer group during the three-year bear market. How did you manage to do that?

Slome: Growth, acceleration, and trends are keys to our stock selection. Early on, compared with other funds, we saw technology companies beginning to underperform. So we reduced our tech exposure, and it benefited our comparative performance. ()

The fund's portfolio holdings mentioned in this article, as of 06/30/04, are: Amazon, xx%; InterActive Corp, x.x%; Teva Pharmaceutical Industries xx%. Holdings are subject to change.

"We are at the start of long-term growth in Internet usage." —Wade Slome

(Profile sent out to thousands of Charles Schwab clients attracted more Ultra investors)

20 Billion Ways to Gather Information

One of the most exciting aspects of managing Ultra was the tremendous access I had to interact with hundreds of brilliant, articulate CEOs, CFOs, Presidents, R&D heads and other executive management team members. When you manage $20+ billion dollars at the touch of your fingertips, executives working in the penthouses of these companies are more than eager to shake your hand with a smile in the hopes that you will peel off some of those fund dollars and invest them in their company's stock. Armed with a large checkbook, these management teams would answer essentially any question I could dream up. If it was a concern of mine, then it became a concern of theirs – since they wanted me to invest.

In what other job could a snot-nosed, 30-something have the gall to ask executives worth dozens of millions (in some cases billions), "Why they overpaid for an acquisition," or "how could you manage to lose money," in a new division. Or in some case, how they could be so greedy, "and sell large amounts of stock," just before a negative news item was released. Regardless of the rainbow of responses, the motivation for the executives was singular: ratchet up the stock price. Maintaining a buoyant stock under the CEO's reign created multiple advantages: 1) An elevated stock price, aided by investor stock purchases, meant that the CEO's wallet could fatten from higher valued option values; 2) Higher stock prices make it easier for companies to attract and retain a higher number of qualified employees; 3) Higher stock prices massage the egos of many executives (who tend to think highly of themselves) and generate free marketing buzz by the journalist community.

Over my years at American Century, I interviewed CEOs (Chief Executive Officers) who controlled companies with cumulative values worth well north of $1,000,000,000,000 ($1 trillion). There was a lot of disparity between the industry and personality types. I held private meetings with everyone from Eric Schmidt (CEO of Google) and Michael Eisner (CEO at Disney) to Lee Scott (Wal-Mart) and Jeff Bezos (Amazon) to name just a few. Other household names included John Chambers (Cisco Systems), Meg Whitman (eBay), Dr. Paul & Irwin Jacobs (Qualcomm), Terry Semel (Yahoo), Arthur Blank and Bernie Marcus (co-founders Home Depot), Hank McKinnell (Pfizer), Mel Karmazin (Sirius & Viacom), Sumner Redstone (Viacom), Michael Dell (Dell Corporation), Tom Stemberg (Staples), among hundreds of others.

The trick to the management interview game was to solicit responses that were different from the canned responses parroted by the companies' legal and marketing departments that CEOs normally regurgitated to dozens of other investors and portfolio managers. Over time, I generated a unique interviewing style that sought to balance the no-nonsense Mike Wallace (60 Minutes) approach with the inquisitive line of questioning of Charlie Rose (The Charlie Rose Show). I even tried to sprinkle in some of Tim Russert's method of unbiased, pressing questions - backed up by endless amounts of facts. "On September 6th you said A-B-C, so why on September 7th did you do X-Y-Z?" Every once in a while I could elicit a deer-in-a-headlight response.

However, coming up with these thoughtful, detailed questions was not easy and required a lot of preparation. But hard work pays off. The more detailed research one does on a company, the more valuable information you get in return. Often I would command a meeting's line of questioning, either due to other professionals' lack of preparedness or their fear of asking a smart billionaire a stupid question. There was a certain satisfaction in seeing these wealthy, smooth and charismatic executives squirm occasionally under difficult questioning or frustratingly hand off a difficult question to an underling. Getting CEOs to drift away from a script was vital because in this game certain information is invaluable, even the reading of body language – which in many cases was louder than the spoken word (very similar to the reading of behavioral "tells" in poker – see Appendix). Getting this information was not easy.

Peers that I worked with often commented on the level of detail and preparation I put into management interviews. Growth master, Phil Fisher, would never meet with management teams without collecting at least 50% of the information needed to make an investment. Or, in other words, he understood that you would only get out of a meeting what you had put into the meeting. As a steward of billions of dollars in capital for individual and institutional investors, I took my job seriously and I know they expected nothing less of me.

Enron, the FBI, and the Art of Slime

Based on the "Law of Large Numbers," I didn't just always get to drill the cream of the crop with questions though. Occasionally I interviewed other executives that scurried around the bottom of the barrel. Jeff Skilling (Enron), Ken Lay (Enron), Bernie Ebbers (Worldcom), Scott Sullivan (Worldcom), Dennis Kozlowski (Tyco), and Hank Greenberg (AIG) are a few controversial personalities that come to mind. Of these previous CEOs, I probably trusted Jeff Skilling the least. He was not the bashful type and he did not stray much from the constant "hard-sell" and had plenty of optimistic forecasts to dish out.

But taking great notes and preparing for management interviews can also create tremendous headaches. Case in point was an incident occurring towards the end of 2003. At that time, my secretary uttered the eight words I never want to hear again, "Hey Wade, the FBI is looking for you." Uggh!

Fortunately for me, the FBI wanted to meet regarding something someone else did – not something I did. Because of the extremely detailed notes that I collected at a January 2000 Enron Analyst Meeting, the FBI wanted information to help send some Enron executives to jail. Surprisingly, based on this event, they were honing in on Kenneth Rice, a senior executive that originally jump started their main energy trading business before transferring over to EBS (Enron Broadband Services). EBS was Enron's response to the convergence of voice, video, and data and the supposed arrival of the "New Economy."

The Enron Analyst Day was very bizarre but still crisp vision in my mind. During a brief break in the frenzied day, I connected with my partners at our home base through a screaming cell phone call, "Hey Wade, what's going on over there at the analyst day? Enron's stock is up over 25%!" Like staging magicians, the Enron event coordinators had orchestrated a grand entrance of Sun Microsystem's CEO, Scott McNealy, who endorsed Enron's grand plan of creating a national broadband data trading network that would allow telecom carriers and ISPs (Internet Service Providers) to buy bandwidth like other commodities, as they needed it. Actually, McNealy was more interested in collecting a check for 18,000 Sun Microsystems sold to Enron rather than explaining the half-baked merits of Enron's bandwidth trading network.

These staged events were all fine until Ken Rice and Jeff Skilling signed off on overly optimistic and unrealistic profitability goals relating to the broadband network. Enron's management went one step further by misleadingly assigning $10-20 billion dollars in value to this money losing venture. Ken Rice was not the type to go down with a sinking ship, so he cunningly sold over one million shares in May 2003 for about $76 million dollars with the knowledge the bandwidth trading network would continue to lose money. Unfortunately for Ken Rice, this is considered insider trading and is what landed the character, Bud Fox, from the movie *Wall Street* in jail. There was a 50% chance that I would have to go to Washington, D.C. and testify as a witness, but fortunately Ken Rice settled for a plea bargain and my services were not required. The money losing bandwidth trading network unit (EBS) was abandoned shortly after Enron's bankruptcy filing in December 2001.

Incidentally, the FBI did an incredible job through my interview processes. As I sat with my company's legal counsel, the investigators went through my notes line by line and asked very thorough, detailed questions. These well-oiled attorneys did not fit the lazy, bureaucratic government employee role stereotyped by many. Hats off to the FBI for doing such a great job and successfully locking up many of the Enron crooks. If there's anything I learned from this experience, it is that next time I go to an analyst day, perhaps I will take less detailed notes – in order to save myself from extensive, straining FBI questioning.

Chapter 7:
Technology & Globalization

In order to fully appreciate the enormity of the Great Pyramids of Egypt, one needs to visit them firsthand. I contest the same principle applies to globalization. One must personally go to areas such as China, India, Brazil, Russia, Dubai and other emerging markets to fully appreciate the scope of demand and growth that will be hitting our global economy in the decades to come. As mentioned earlier, I have been afforded the opportunity to visit around 25 countries on five continents over my lifetime. My thirst to explore many new locations still has not been quenched. These experiences and relationships helped to open a whole new point of view relating to the inter-connection of markets and the role that culture, politics, and economics play in globalization. In order to take advantage of long-term, multi-year global investment trends, I am convinced that consistent, sustainable profits are unachievable without a broad multi-dimensional analysis that takes into account factors such as culture, politics, and economics. Ignoring a leg of this three-legged stool will ultimately lead to the investment toppling.

Globalization, "Denver" Style

I experienced my most surreal globalization moment while I was visiting Beijing, China, in March 2005. There we were, a group of wide-eyed investors from the U.S., soaking in the atmosphere at a local bar in a club district of Beijing. Tom Nguyen, our chaperone from Deutsche Bank Securities, naively asked, "I wonder what the market's doing?" Well, since it was nearly midnight and we were across the world, the U.S. equity markets were still open for a few hours back on the other half of the world. I don't think Alexander Graham Bell had this in mind when he created telephone lines; but before I knew it, I was texting a colleague in Kansas City, Missouri, on my Blackberry with one hand, while drinking a Dutch-brewed Heineken with the other hand. But wait -- it gets stranger. As I completed my text message, I gently raised my head and realized that a native, female Chinese singer was belting out John Denver's country classic, "Rocky Mountain High", in a garbled English speaking voice that surprisingly was still much clearer and more coherent than my beer-laden, jetlagged voice. Anybody that says China doesn't embrace "capitalism" needs to pound the pavement in Beijing and experience country music Chinese style.

(Beijing's version of Britney Spears singing John Denver's *Rocky Mountain High*)

Globalization and free trade is not a new concept. Adam Smith, the father of modern economics, wrote about "Comparative Advantage" in 1776, when he wrote *Wealth of Nations*. He wrote, "If a foreign country can supply us with a commodity cheaper than we ourselves can make it, better buy it of them with some part of the produce of our own industry, employed in a way in which we have some advantage." Politics has repeatedly tried to slow the evolution of globalization, outsourcing, and free trade. Certainly jobs can and will be lost due to these trends; however, in order to survive in our global economy, our companies need to maximize efficiency. Healthier corporations will have the financial resources to create higher paying and more productive jobs. If isolationist and protectionist policies reign supreme, then I believe our country's leadership positions across various industries will slowly atrophy away as ambitious, growth-oriented, open societies embrace the more effective rules of globalization.

New Chinese Capitalism

The 20th century was the century of the United States and odds are favoring China as the leader of the 21st Century. China has a population that is more than four times larger than the U.S. population (~1.3 billion vs. ~300 million), but the U.S. has a GDP (Gross Domestic Product) that is four times larger than China's GDP (~$13.8 trillion in 2007 vs. ~$3.3 trillion).

(Now I know what Yao Ming feels like! These students thought I had come from a freak show and wanted to take a picture with me).

Sure, the Chinese practice a different version of democracy than we Americans are accustomed to, but if you were in charge of hundreds of millions of impoverished Chinese peasants and feared a lower-class revolution, you might want to keep a tighter leash on your people too. Tremendous advancements in openness have occurred over the last few decades since the 1989 Tiananmen Square protests and subsequent massacre. China's inclusion into the World Trade Organization in 2001 was a watershed event. For heaven's sake, China has a chain of Hooters! In October 2004, Hooters restaurant opened its first outlet in China, bringing its combination of cold beer, chicken wings and skimpily dressed waitresses to one of the world's fastest growing economies.

Noted New York Times journalist, Thomas Friedman, wrote about his famous "Golden Arches Theory of Conflict Prevention" which basically said that no two countries with a McDonald's franchise had ever gone to war with one another. The premise behind this belief was that as countries embrace technology and the productivity benefits derived from these systems, standards of living rise to levels that countries do not want to jeopardize by going to war. With the NATO bombings of Serbia and the recent skirmish of Russia invading Georgia, perhaps this theory has been compromised and a new "Hooters Tube-Top Theory of Conflict Prevention" needs to be instituted!

There are definitely advantages to the "westernization" of Asia, but there definitely are some trade-offs as well. As 20 million people per year are moving from rural farming towns to the urban cities, death rates are increasing in China due to such factors as stress, less exercise, more fast food (especially Kentucky Fried Chicken (KFC) which is opening more Chinese restaurants than American stores) and pollution. The associated damage caused by industrialization and 'global warming' is accelerating the spread of desert expansion too, as roughly 25% of China's geography is classified as desert climate and the figure is still growing.

Regardless of your political beliefs, money has a mind of its own. Quite simply put, money or capital migrates to locations where it is treated best. Generally this means that countries that can grow the fastest, balance economic destroyers (i.e. inflation, taxes) and maintain political stability will attract the most capital.

So how do countries grow faster? I argue that the U.S., through capitalism and its superior democratic system, has created a unique and unrivaled breeding ground for entrepreneurial innovation. Sure there is room for a lot of improvement, but the U.S. has managed to out-innovate our global brethren through advanced use of technology. Everything from Qualcomm (QCOM) CDMA 3G chips to networking routers at Cisco Systems (CSCO) are raising living standards globally. The 44 year chart below highlights the rising importance that technology plays in our economy and neighboring countries are slowly figuring out this secret.

Tech Spend as % of GDP

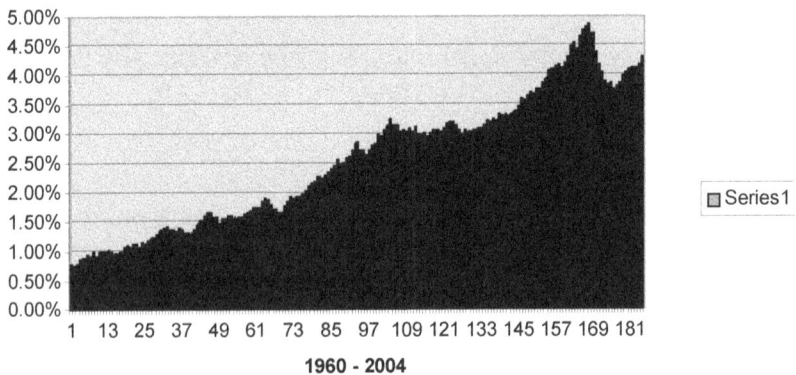

(Data created by Bear Stearns Research Department (May 2005))

This is not a new trend. The cavemen innovated in the Stone Age through the creation of advanced tools. Later on in history, Johannes Gutenberg (1455) revolutionized the storage, transfer and replication of information through the Gutenberg Press (the paper version of the Internet). During the late 18th - early 19th century, the 'Industrial Revolution' began in Britain then spread throughout the world and replaced muscles with steam. The applications of the steam engine were incredible and the possibilities virtually endless. The 'Rail Revolution' became a natural outcome of the 'Industrial Revolution' and created an unrivaled period of economic prosperity. Innovation obviously did not stop there. Where would we be without our good friends, Orville & Wilbur Wright, who crashed their first human flight in 1903? Or would we have the choices between the likes of Lamborghinis and Rolls Royces today without Henry Ford's manufacturing skill in creating the Model T (priced at $950 in 1908)?

In a world of TiVos (Digital Video Recorders), 3G iPhones (3rd Generation), GPS (Global Positioning System) devices, Wi-Fi (Wireless Fidelity internet connection), paperless/digital offices, and more, many people of my generation have lost sight of the simple pleasures gained over the last four decades. For example, our kids will never know what it was like to live without a microwave. Or the pleasures of owning a VHS recorder the size of an ice chest (not to mention the obsolete dinosaur called Betamax). Will our children sympathize with the brick-sized mobile phones we sherpa'd around? How about life before the

Internet? Oh, how technology has changed our lives, even over such a short time frame. As you can see from the chart below, almost 25% of the world's population now has access to the Internet.

Internet Users in the World
March 2008

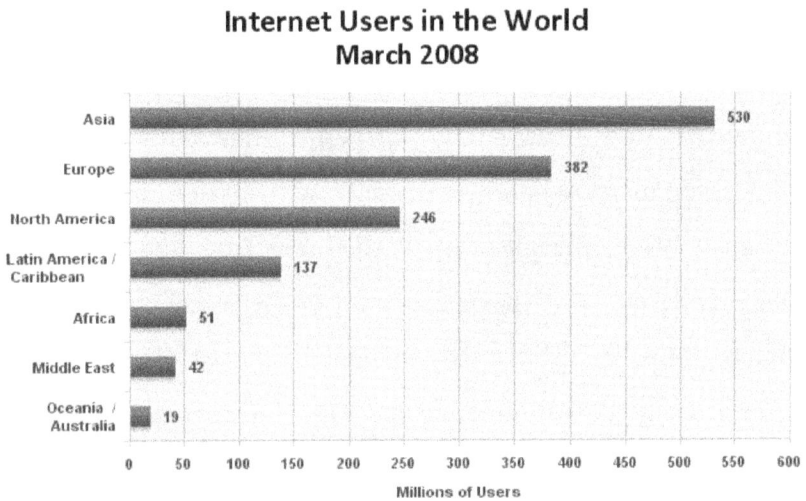

Note: World Internet Users estimate is 1,407,724,920 for Q1 2008
Copyright © 2008, Miniwatts Marketing Group - www.internetworldstats.com

Trade Deficit and Margin Surplus

There has been a lot of trade deficit bashing going on in recent years along with the concurrently sounding currency alarms. The press and Warren Buffett have been directly linking the trade deficit with the declining U.S. dollar. This is one area where I think Buffett's critical comments are missing the boat and distorting reality. Sure, we have recently experienced a decline in the U.S. dollar, but the real question becomes is this due to trade deficits or other reasons? Andy Kessler, former hedge fund manager and author of *Running Money*, summed it up perfectly when he described the U.S. "margin surplus" and explained this phenomenon via the import of a $1,000 Toshiba Japanese laptop computer to the United States. His rough math shows that about $350 of that laptop's value can be attributed to high-value U.S. components and software (Intel microprocessor and Microsoft Windows Operating System), so therefore a $650 net trade deficit has been created ($1,000-$350) from a laptop purchase in the U.S. What this analysis neglects to address is the relative profits created from both sides of this import-export example. Although the laptop shipment produced a higher import ($650) sales value, the gross profit to Toshiba is only $50 due to the commodity nature of the Japanese components. On the other hand, the main U.S. components/software sold for $350, but it created more than $300 in U.S.-based profits. I will take a six-fold increase in profits ($300 vs. $50) in exchange for a $650 higher trade deficit all day and twice on Sunday.

Another real-life Slome household example is evident from a quick scan of my apple iPhone. Flip over the device and on the back you can read: *Designed by Apple in California Assembled in China.* Again, who do you think is making more money from these products, the U.S. company with a $150 billion market capitalization or the Chinese assembly workers making a few dollars per day? Perhaps Mr. Buffett should bark up the tree of expanding budget deficits, protectionist trade policies, or fiscal monetary policies when explaining the decline in the U.S. dollar – not trade deficits.

Rise of the Rest

What all these globalization examples show me are that countries are becoming more and more interconnected and technology is accelerating this trend. As a result of globalization, millions of impoverished people in emerging markets are ascending out of poverty and joining an exploding global middle class. Economic trade and growth still remain the best anti-poverty programs. Fareed Zakaria, *Newsweek* journalist, points out that in 2006 and 2007, 124 countries grew their economies at over four percent a year (including 30 countries in Africa). The U.S. can choose to embrace this trend and maintain our large lead in the global race or we can put on blinders and let other countries catch us (or pass us) in this long marathon. Tom Friedman, *NY Times* columnist, points out that hundreds of thousands of lower paying tax-return, data-entry jobs have been exported to India and the numbers are growing rapidly. As more efficient U.S. companies become more profitable, it behooves them to invest in higher paying job areas that our international brethren are not capable of duplicating, so that we will be more competitive in the global markets. How the U.S. reacts to this accelerating trend of globalization will determine whether what Mr. Zakaria calls the "Rise of the Rest" will be a threat or an opportunity for the United States. Mr. Friedman jokes that, "My mom told me to eat my dinner because there are starving children in China and India – I tell my kids to do their homework because Chinese and Indians are starving for their jobs." Time to crack the homework whip on my daughter!

Chapter 8: Winning Strategies

Longer Time Horizons & Compounding

If you are constantly changing bait and swapping your fishing line in and out of the lake, then catching fish becomes much tougher. I make the case that the same principle applies to investing in stocks. Just take a look to see how the S&P 500 performed over the last 50 years under an index strategy that has long investment time horizons (low portfolio turnover). The index is up more than 20-fold! Not too shabby [see S&P 500 chart later in this chapter]. And this performance was achieved despite horrendous events that impacted the market, including recessions, SARs, wars, assassinations, currency crises, terrorist attacks, technology bubbles, 'Mad Cow' disease, accounting scandals, and now a bursting real estate bubble. Earnings are cyclical but the trend, like stock prices, eventually moves up and to the right. My belief that price follows earnings has already been established; so by keeping the fishing line in the water, investors can maximize the power of compounding – a concept embraced by my friend, Albert Einstein. Phil Fisher's following statement is extreme, "If the job has been correctly done when a common stock is purchased, the time to sell it is – almost never"; however, I agree with it directionally.

The market has not done much over the last ten years despite the significant rise in earnings from 1998 to mid 2008. If earnings are going up, and prices are staying steady, then we should infer that valuation multiples are compressing and stocks overall are becoming more attractive in value.

S&P 500 Index & Major Global Events
(Jan 1963 – Jun 2008)

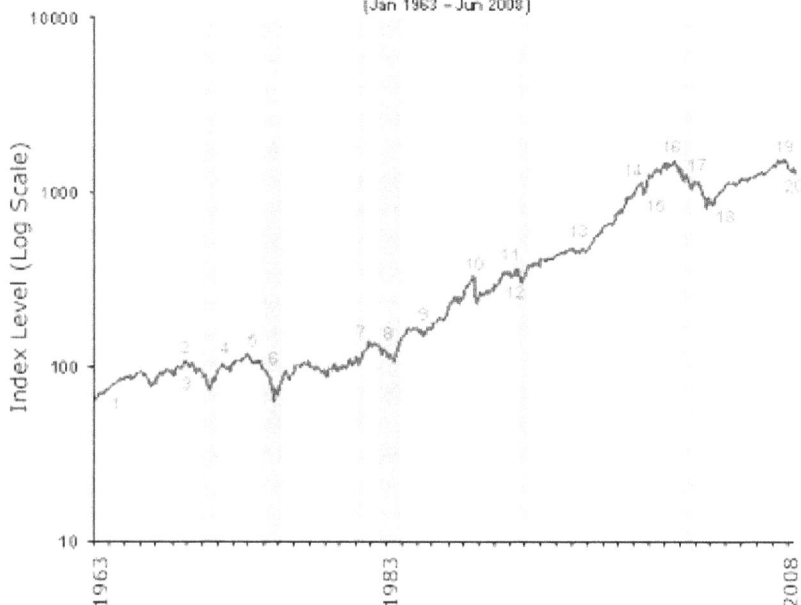

1 JFK Assassination	1963	11 U.S. Savings and Loan Crisis	1989
2 Vietnam - Tet Offensive	1968	12 Persian Gulf War	1990
3 MLK, RFK Assassinations	1968	13 Mexican Peso Crisis	1994
4 Dollar-Gold Convertibility	1971	14 Asian Financial Crisis	1997
5 OPEC Oil Embargo	1973	15 LTCM² Collapse	1998
6 Watergate - Nixon Resigns	1974	16 Tech/Internet Bubble Burst	2000
7 Iranian Revolution-Oil Crisis	1979	17 9-11	2001
8 Latin American Debt Crisis	1982	18 Iraq War	2003
9 Continental Illinois Collapse	1984	19 Subprime Mortgage Crisis	2007
10 Black Monday	1987	20 Bear Stearns Collapse	2008

(U.S. stocks have proven to be durable over the long term. For illustrative purposes, Fidelity Investments showed that a $10,000 hypothetical investment in a strategy mimicking the S&P 500 index from 1963 would have increased in value to $865,000 by the end of June 2008. Shaded regions represent U.S. recessions as defined by the National Bureau of Economic Research. The chart is created on a logarithmic scale, whereby distances are represented by equal ratios.)

(Christopher Columbus in some dapper 15th Century clothes)

Columbus Compounding

Why is compounding so great? Albert Einstein, whom we discussed earlier and is arguably one of the most intelligent people who ever lived, was asked to describe mankind's greatest discovery. His answer: "compound interest." He went so far as to call it the 'Eighth Wonder of the World.' The benefits of compounding can be demonstrated through a simple example using famous explorer, Christopher Columbus.

We all know the story, "In 1492, Christopher Columbus sailed the ocean blue!" To emphasize the benefits of compounding, let us suppose that Christopher Columbus made an investment in the new world's future in the historic year of 1492. If Chris had placed a single penny in a 6% interest-bearing account and instructed someone to remove the interest every year, the value of the interest earned through 2008 would be almost 31 cents. A pretty nice multiplier-effect on one penny, but not too much absolute cold hard cash to write home about...agreed?

However, if the young explorer had placed the same paltry investment of one cent into the same interest-bearing account, but LEFT the remaining earned interest to compound (thereby earning interest upon the interest) the results would be drastically different.

What would you guess the account would be worth now? $10,000? $100,000? $1 million? $10 million? $100 million? NO is the answer to all these guesses.

The correct answer: $114,242,178,628.50!! Your eyes are not deceiving you. That one penny invested in 1492 would have grown to $114 billion dollars. Surely, we will not live 516 years to collect on any investment over such a long duration; however most investors have the ability to invest quite a bit more than one cent.

More modern day evidence of the power of compounding may be discovered by analyzing T. Rowe Price, the very skilled Growth investor. In the 1970s, he held Xerox (XRX) which increased by an astounding 6,184% rate over a 12 year period. His investment in drug giant Merck gained an eye-popping +23,666% over the 31 years that he owned it.

When it comes to stocks, companies that can sustainably grow earnings at 15-20% annually will double earnings in approximately three to five years, meaning that price appreciation should, on average, double over the same time frame – not bad returns if you can identify them. Achieving the advantage of compounding is difficult to achieve if one is constantly trading and speculating through the barrage of news clutter in the marketplace. With 75% of active funds underperforming the index over time, I believe that my competitive advantage is NOT being a better trader versus the thousands and thousands hedge fund and buy-side competitors. I strongly believe it is better to tuck your core portfolio away and integrate tactical enhancements that use volatility as a friend (trim on spikes and nibble on implosions). However, for the most part, let your portfolio do the heavy lifting for you.

One reason trading frequency has risen and time horizons have shortened is because, thanks to heightened electronic trading, costs have come down dramatically. Large institutional managers (think of Fidelity, Vanguard, American Funds, etc.), in certain cases, are paying less than one penny per share for trades.

Therefore a purchase of 10,000 shares may cost less than $100 in commissions. Currently, larger established retail brokerage firms like Scottrade and Fidelity charge as low as $7 - $8 per trade. Although the trend in costs is coming down, we cannot forget about the negative effects of bid-ask spreads and trading impact costs.

Regardless of the costs, each situation needs to be judged rationally. If the benefits of trading look to outweigh the costs, then turnover should increase to exploit these inefficiencies. In certain environments, there will simply be more opportunities and will require more trading activity – both on the long and short side. Keep in mind, as I mentioned earlier, each trade transaction (no matter how cheap) requires investors to be right twice on both sides of the trade (buy and sell). Moreover, often the emotional costs create a heavier toll than the lower transaction costs. So the moral of the story is that most people only account for the explicit commission costs when analyzing total trading costs, when realistically there are a host of other unaccounted tangible/intangible costs.

John Bogle proved investors have a difficult time keeping pace with professional managers and perform even worse than passive index strategies. The index outperformed the average investor by more than 10% over the 18 year period studied below (see chart below). "People always seem to buy today what they should have bought about five years earlier," observed Bill Miller. It was not unusual to see an average investor get suckered into buying a hot five-star tech fund at the peak of the market in 2000, only to sell 70% lower 18 months later and witness the proceeds sit 100% in low-yielding cash. Of course the market bottomed shortly thereafter, and the S&P 500 and NASDAQ (National Association of Securities Dealers Automated Quotation System) indexes more than doubled over the next five years. Two words: whipsaw city!

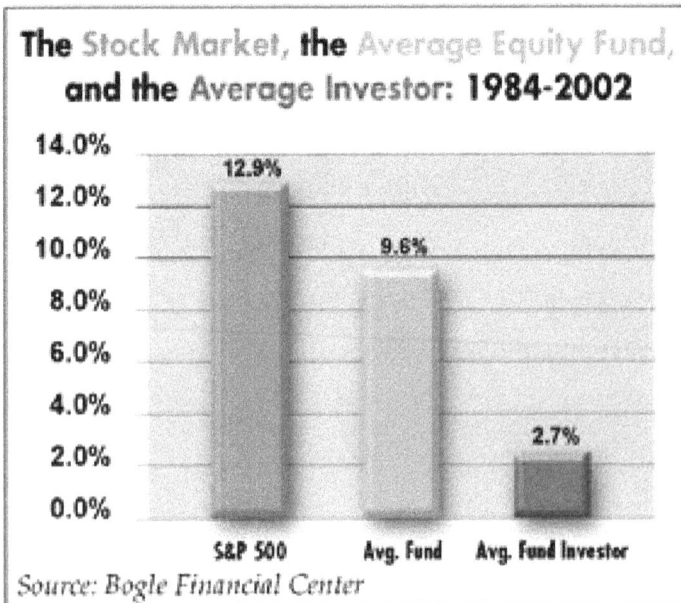

The Stock Market, **the** Average Equity Fund, **and the** Average Investor: 1984-2002

S&P 500	Avg. Fund	Avg. Fund Investor
12.9%	9.6%	2.7%

Source: Bogle Financial Center

Past performance is no guarantee of future results.

Long Term Diversification

With the life expectancies of people extending out to 90-100+ years old, the risk of outliving your retirement savings becomes a larger reality and forces people to embrace the concept of compounding more seriously. You can see below that equities as measured by the S&P 500 have been a great area to have exposure over the last 50 years, despite a healthy level of volatility. Certainly each investor should sit down with an advisor or come up with a diversified strategy across asset classes and geographic regions (subject to risk tolerances and retirement objectives).

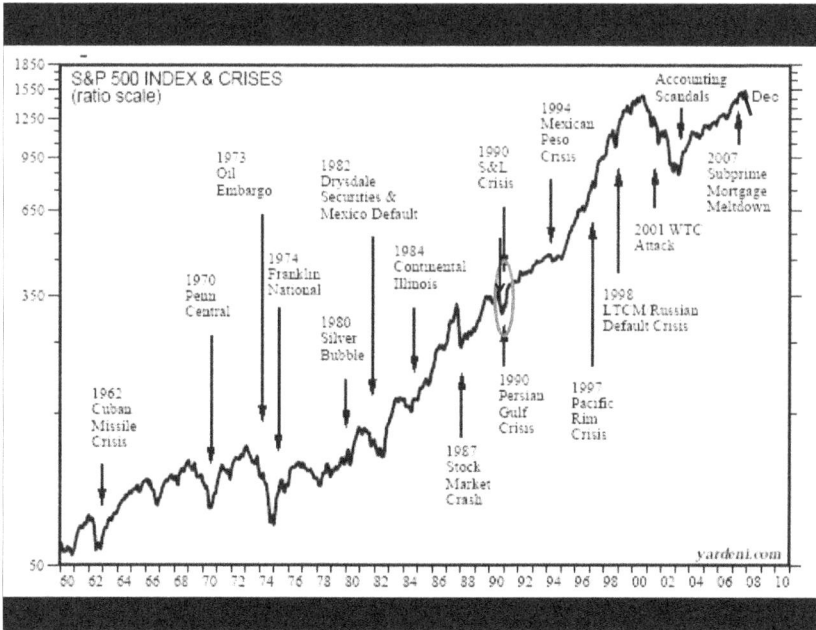

Considering my longer term investment horizon, I make every effort to exploit extraneous short term volatility in exchange for better purchase/sale prices. A reasonable level of expected turnover I target is between 20% and 33%. Here is Mr. Lynch's astute observation on the subject: "Whatever method you use to pick stocks or stock mutual funds, your ultimate success or failure will depend on your ability to ignore the worries of the world long enough to allow your investments to succeed."

Writing Options

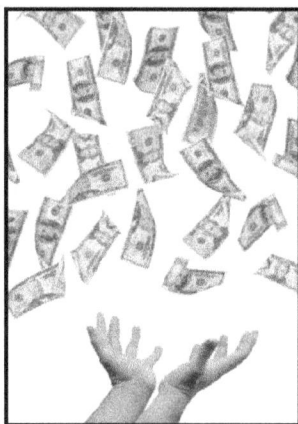

How would you like to collect free money for something you wanted to do anyway?

Let's suppose my friend, Ken, is a Batman fanatic and has a ticket to go see the movie *Dark Knight* at the 'drive-in' tonight. I have yet to see it, and really want to see it. The only issue is that

Ken has a convertible and it might rain tonight (I have a comfy SUV with power wipers). So when Ken offers up the following proposition: "I'll pay you $3 bucks to buy my *Dark Knight* ticket if it rains tonight." I say, "O.K. buddy, you give me the $3 bucks right now, rain or shine, and you gotta deal!" What a bargain! I want to go see the movie anyway, so if it rains I get $3 extra bucks to buy soda and popcorn at the drive-in. And if it doesn't rain, I get to keep the $3 and buy a quart of Ben & Jerry's and woof it down while I watch one of my favorite movies *Memento* (another movie directed by Christopher Nolan!) in the comfort of my own home.

What I just described above was how I effectively "wrote a put option" (sold an option) on the possibility of buying a movie ticket. As crazy as the scenario sounds, you should have seen the crazy options and other customized derivatives that the Wall Street investment banks like Goldman Sachs, Merrill Lynch, and Lehman Brothers dreamt up every day. And you won't be surprised that the banks made a healthy cut (like a bookie) for each transaction, whether it rained or shined.

When it comes to writing (selling) put options on stock positions, one collects premiums upfront based on the event of a stock reaching a certain price level. Typically, the put option transaction occurs with a strike price (trigger price) that is currently below the current market price. Let us take Google stock (ticker symbol: GOOG) for example. For instance, suppose the current price of GOOG shares (in September) were trading at $600 per share, and I liked GOOG but did not currently own the shares. However, although I like it now, I really would <u>LOVE</u> to buy GOOG at $400 (I like things on sale!). In addition, the current premium offered on a share of GOOG stock with a strike price (trigger price) of $400 (in the month of December) is currently yielding $9.50.

Given the scenario above (GOOG shares currently at $600 in September and strike/trigger at $400 in December), I may consider writing (selling) a PUT option on GOOG shares and collect the $9.50 today. Just as in the *Dark Knight* movie ticket example, I am getting paid free money today for something I want to do anyway.

So where is the catch? Well, allow us to consider the situation where GOOG stock goes from $600 in September to $300 in December. Since the strike (trigger) price was $400, as the stock cratered, I was forced to buy the GOOG shares at $400 and realize the difference in price of $100 ($400 stock price – [minus] new $300 price in December). The optimist in me says, well at least I did not lose the whole $300 ($600 September price -$300 December price) and I also collected and kept the $9.50 up front to buffer my $100 realized loss. If GOOG shares end up trading at $401 or $1,000 per share in December, I am NOT forced to buy any GOOG shares and I get to KEEP the initial $9.50 in premium.

These examples are awfully simplistic and do not include many important details, but they do highlight a strategy that can be effective in volatile market periods. As volatility increases, the premiums collected at the front of options transactions become even larger (i.e. the $9.50 might jump to $12-$13?) so that investors can profit from volatility and continue implementing their planned investment strategies.

I did not go over writing (selling) 'call' options, but the previous mechanics simply work in reverse. Unlike writing a put option when I am forced to buy stock if the stock price falls below the strike (trigger) price, in writing a call option I am forced to sell a stock if the price rises above a strike (trigger) price. Since writing naked calls involves limitless potential losses, I encourage most investors to stick to writing 'covered calls'. Basically, this strategy allows a person holding a stock to collect upfront premiums today and subsequently be forced to sell a stock IF the price reaches a certain strike price (usually above the current price) by a certain date.

Another area I did not discuss was buying options (puts or calls). Since these strategies COST money (no free money coming my way) and are not consistent with my investment philosophy, I will not go into detail on these strategies. In short, buying options is an employed strategy that is used as insurance on stocks you own, or buying options is used as a leveraged strategy to amplify returns based on relatively short time-framed price swings. In most cases I would prefer collecting premiums from these short-term, price-volatility speculators (write options), rather than paying premiums (buy options).

So there you have it, you are now options writing experts and can start collecting that free money falling from the sky!

Tool-belt

Chapter 4 discussed my investment philosophy and this chapter reviewed strategies emanating from those core beliefs. The strategies discussed ranged from exploiting short-term price volatility through premium collections (writing options) and weather-proofing portfolios by allocating assets into low-cost, tax-efficient vehicles such as ETFs (Exchange Traded Funds). An ETF effectively is an index fund that can be purchased or shorted during a day of trading. A typical index fund, like an open-ended fund, requires the investor to trade only AFTER the close of daily trading. Regardless, these short-term and long-term winning strategies will serve as valuable tools in helping investors achieve higher, compounded, risk-adjusted returns.

Chapter 9: Choosing an Investment Manager & Advisor

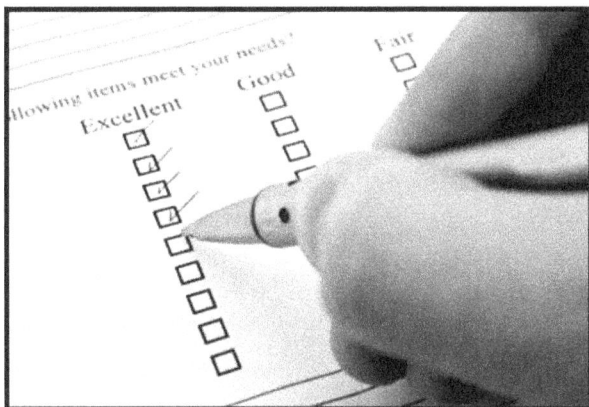

Your financial future is important. And if you are a busy professional who has little to no time to handle your financial matters, then you are a prime candidate to outsource these responsibilities to a professional investment manager or advisor. If you are willing to outsource the relatively meaningless responsibilities of landscaping, car washes, house cleaning, etc., then why would successful professionals with insufficient time to floss their teeth make half-baked investment decisions that may compromise their financial futures? However, for those individuals that could use the assistance of a professional advisor, they should not take this decision lightly. Here are a few areas that the client should seriously review when it comes to selecting an investment manager or advisor.

Experience

Would you want a nurse handling your brain surgery? Would you want a flight attendant flying your plane? Most rational people respond with just one answer, and that is with a resounding NO! The reason being...experience counts. When selecting an advisor or investment professional the importance of credentials is paramount (see also Chapter 10). The licensing process is not overly taxing when it comes to security industry registration, therefore it behooves potential clients to perform the proper due diligence when contemplating the engagement of a new advisor's services.

Services Offered

If the scope of the client's needs go beyond investment management, then it is incumbent upon the client to determine whether the advisor is capable of offering the desired services. In many instances, the advisor may lack the experience or know-how to service the client's needs. Business owners and entrepreneurs can have complex problems that require a breadth of knowledge that exceeds the scope of services offered by the advisor.

Fees/Commissions

(Make sure your investment/manager is charging reasonable fees and/or commissions)

It is important to know what an investment manager or advisor is charging you in fees and/or commissions. Often clients are unaware of buried fee language in the small-print of thick legal documents. By directly asking your investment professional how he/she is getting paid, you can remove ambiguity that may exist.

I recently reviewed a Variable Life Policy from an unnamed carrier that included the following charges:

- A hefty 12% 'Premium Charge' that was deducted monthly. These charges appear similar in some respects to 12b-1 fees charged to investors in the mutual fund industry because Premium Charges are designed to defray sales and tax expenses incurred in relation to the premium payments.

- Drastic 'Surrender Charges' that approached $100,000 in the early years of the policy on a $2 million death benefit, which effectively lock the insured into owning the policy and paying premiums. Of course the insured can stop paying the premiums, but will be forced to forgo the Cash Value in the policy that has already built up. Cash Value is the investment component of certain life insurance policies that can grow tax deferred until withdrawn from the account.

- "Cost of Insurance Charge" that goes up every year, and theoretically can exceed the premium payments, if the insured lives past a certain age, in which case the Cash Value of the policy would be reduced to cover the rising insurance charges.

- The "Mortality and Expense Charge" is another layer of fees spread over the other expenses. In this case, an additional 1.75% in annualized fees was being deducted monthly with the ability to increase at the carrier's choice.

- But wait, there's more. The insured does not get a set of Ginsu knives, but rather receives the privilege of paying added monthly 'Administrative Charges' that equate to $240 per year.

- Well, that covers the insurance charges I discovered, but when it comes to the investment side of the equation, there are other extra fees and expenses deducted from the Variable Life policy such as the following:
  a. 'Management Fees'
  b. '12b-1 Fees'
  c. 'Legal/Accounting Fees'
  d. 'Brokerage Commissions'
  e. And second born child (just kidding)

Suffice it to say, whether it is mutual funds, stocks, insurance, or other financial products, there are plenty of fees that many investors/policy owners are unaware of due to lack of transparency in the sales process. In certain situations, the advisor pushing a product has a financial incentive to sell a certain product – unless the client asks questions they will remain in the dark when it comes to conflicts of interest.

When it comes to investment management, there is a slow but predictable trend toward 'Fee-Only' advisors. Sidoxia Capital Management, like other 'Fee-Only' advisors, charges fees as a percentage of assets under management. Therefore the investment advisor has a vested interest in client assets appreciating. If client assets decline, the advisor's paycheck is reduced. In the commission based world of many brokerage firms, the broker/advisor can collect robust commissions at the front-end of a transaction and as a result of hitting sales driven quotas may enjoy a trip to the Bahamas. If the client's investments do not perform, then oh well - no big deal - the broker has already collected his commission. Perhaps the client will get a postcard from the Caribbean?

Advisor Approach & Process
When talking about the investment process, too often smoke and mirrors are used in the client-advisor engagement process. A flurry of acronyms and buzz words are used by the advisor as a way of displaying their definitional prowess. Usually a tree or two has been killed to produce a meaningless mound of paper in the form of an indecipherable financial plan or glossy marketing brochure, none of which helps the client understand how their money will be invested.

Ideally advisors will walk the client through their approach in an educational, easy-to-understand manner. But, unfortunately, too often the client comes out of a meeting pulling out his hair, wondering what all those confusing investment terms meant. If the advisor does not take the initiative in explaining their philosophical approach and process, then it is essential that the client step in to ask questions.

When the advice purchaser is confused, no matter how awkward or embarrassing it may feel, there is nothing wrong with asking, "What does that mean?" or "Why would you implement that approach?" The client is typically spending thousands of dollars for this critical, life impacting financial advice and should not feel uncomfortable in asking simple questions. When pondering this topic, I always reminisce back to the sage advice frequently reiterated by my 2nd grade teacher, Mrs. Leichenring, "There is no such thing as a dumb question." If your advisor belittles your questions or gives you a hard time, I suggest you consider finding an advisor who respects your concerns.

Review Background
There is so much crime and fraud happening in today's society that it is imperative for investors to make sure the investment manager or advisor who is hired has a squeaky clean record. Getting referrals from trusted sources is one way of limiting risk,

yet there are additional resources available on line to check manager/advisor backgrounds. With proper research, investors can become more comfortable with the professional chosen and the status of the firm employing the manager/professional.

Several government and professional regulatory organizations, such as the National Association of Securities Dealers (NASD), the Securities & Exchange Commission (SEC), your state insurance and securities departments, and CFP Board keep records on the disciplinary history of the investment and financial planning advisors. Ask what organizations the professional is regulated by and contact these groups to conduct a background check.

Here are a few links that you may reference:

FINRA (Financial Industry Regulatory Authority)

http://www.finra.org/InvestorInformation/InvestorProtection/Ch ecktheBackgroundofYourInvestmentProfessional/index.htm

SEC (Securities and Exchange Commission)

http://www.adviserinfo.sec.gov/IAPD/Content/Search/iapd_Org Search.aspx

Chapter 10: Credentials & Education

When reviewing the credentials of an advisor there are a host of questions that need to be asked. First of all, does he/she have a college degree, and if so, from where and which degree? A degree from North South East e-Learners.com University in 'Philosophy' probably doesn't hold the same weight as a 'Business' or 'Economics' degree from an accredited institution. Does he/she hold any other investment or financial planning credentials such as the highly regarded CFA (Chartered Financial Analyst) and CFP® (Certified Financial Planner) designations? There is an alphabet soup full of letters that are attached to peoples' names, but when it comes to the investment field, no other letters are held with the same esteem as the CFA & CFP® credentials. Although not required, does the advisor have a master's degree? When dealing with your personal money, why not be selective in choosing the person that will be managing your treasured assets?

As implied above, not all letters are created equal. Very few combinations of letters establish such professional credibility as the CFA (Chartered Financial Analyst) and CFP® (Certified Financial Planner) designations. It is estimated that less than 10% of all advisors have a CFP®, and less than 5% of all advisors have both the CFA and CFP® designations. Extensive amounts of materials must be mastered to receive the CFA designation and CFP® certification.

The CFP® curriculum can be found in 300 undergraduate, graduate, and certificate programs in 190 colleges and universities. The CFA curriculum has been adopted by 11 universities including the University of Chicago, Harvard, and Yale, and other universities are currently in the process of adoption or consideration of adoption.

The CFA designation and CFP® certification are voluntary designations that are not required by regulators to perform the general duties of financial professionals.

CFA (Chartered Financial Analyst)

The Chartered Financial Analyst (CFA) designation is regarded by most industry participants to be the premier certification for investment management professionals. Candidates for the CFA designation must pass three rigorous, six-hour exams over at least two years, have a minimum of three years of professional investment experience, and commit to abide by the CFA Institute's Code of Ethics and Standards of Professional Conduct.

The CFA exam tests graduate-level knowledge of:

- Investment analysis
- Portfolio management
- Financial statement analysis
- Corporate finance
- Economics
- Performance measurement
- Professional ethics

Typically, 750 hours of study-time, prior to each of the three annual exam dates, is required to pass. Thus, CFA charterholders have demonstrated a commitment to achieving the highest level of skill and knowledge to better serve their clients.

Both the CFA and CFP® have education requirements, testing requirements, and experience requirements necessary for designation approval.

CFP® (CERTIFIED FINANCIAL PLANNER)

CFP® practitioners must pass a comprehensive two-day, ten-hour CFP® Certification Examination that tests their ability to apply financial planning knowledge in an integrated format. CFP® professionals must have three years minimum experience in the financial planning process prior to earning the right to use the CFP® certification marks.

Prerequisites for the CFP® exam include a bachelor's degree and completion of a CFP® Board-registered education program, which includes over 100 financial planning topics. This education program is typically completed in 18-24 months. In addition to these prerequisites, it is estimated that over 300 hours of exam preparation is required.

After completing the education, examination, and experience components, a minimum of 30 hours of continuing education every two years must be completed, along with an agreement to adhere to the CFP® Board's Code of Ethics and Professional Responsibility and Financial Planning Practice Standards. These standards set forth the advisor's ethical responsibilities to the public, clients and employers. The CFP® Board also performs a background check during this process, and each individual must disclose any investigations or legal proceedings related to their professional or business conduct.

Remember, your investment advisor can never be too educated or have too much experience to invest your hard earned savings and retirement money, so make certain that he/she has the proper qualifications.

Chapter 11: What to Do with Your Portfolio

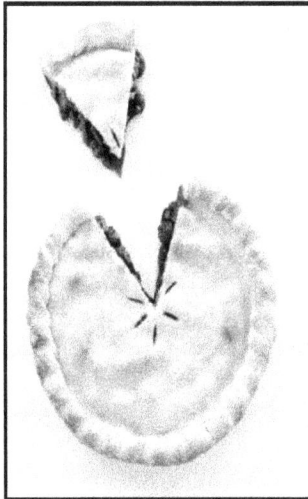

Having read through the majority of this book, you are now armed with the knowledge to make better investment decisions. But before you plunge in, you must first have a clearer understanding of your risk tolerance in conjunction with your current objectives and circumstances. A single 26-year-old teacher will have and need a different investment portfolio as compared to a 63-year-old CEO of a publicly traded company. Each situation requires careful consideration and a thorough review.

Diversification

A common thread that should be evident across portfolios is diversification. During 2008, we have experienced firsthand the need for diversification in what have traditionally been classified as conservative asset classes. Bank failures, such as IndyMac (third largest in U.S. history), have proved the necessity to spread our capital across numerous banks and/or different checking/money market/savings accounts to retain the necessary levels below the $100,000 FDIC insured limits. The ARS (Auction Rate Security) debacle that locked up billions of dollars and generated billions of dollar losses for the investment banks and account holders has demonstrated the benefits of spreading our investments around – even for those secure retirees that are focused primarily on wealth preservation.

Low Cost, Tax-Efficiency

The other theme repeated throughout this book is the importance of low-cost, tax-efficient strategies that integrate longer term investment horizons. The "low-cost" component can come from several areas, including index funds, ETFs (Exchange Traded Funds), and individual security purchases through discount trading intermediaries. The "tax-efficient" aspects of investing can be achieved through tax-smart strategies and tax-smart products. On the strategy front, tax-loss harvesting can be a tremendous tool to utilize when this practice aligns with the investment thesis and is consistent with maximizing long-term after-tax returns. Longer term investment horizons not only benefit the realization of lower capital gains tax rates, but they also provide the benefits of compounding price appreciation (see Chapter 8: Winning Strategies). Go figure, the "low cost" products are also the "tax-efficient products" – index funds, ETFs, and individual securities held for greater than 12 months.

Unfortunately, the picture is not complete by merely employing a diversified portfolio utilizing low-cost, tax-efficient vehicles. A disciplined process and plan needs to be applied that can serve as an emotionless blueprint in periods of market volatility. Investment managers and advisors exploit a wide array of processes. I argue that a herd-following process that buys what's hot and sells what's not, will only lead to failure. I strongly believe that a systematic approach that "buys fear and sells greed" in dynamically growing companies and industries will succeed over time. Just as in most professions, investing requires a great deal of time and focus to achieve success. There are a certain number of independent investors that have the time and discipline to handle their investments. For many others, I suggest that you focus on what you do the "best" (your profession) and outsource the "rest" to a professional advisor.

Fear or Greed in the Market?

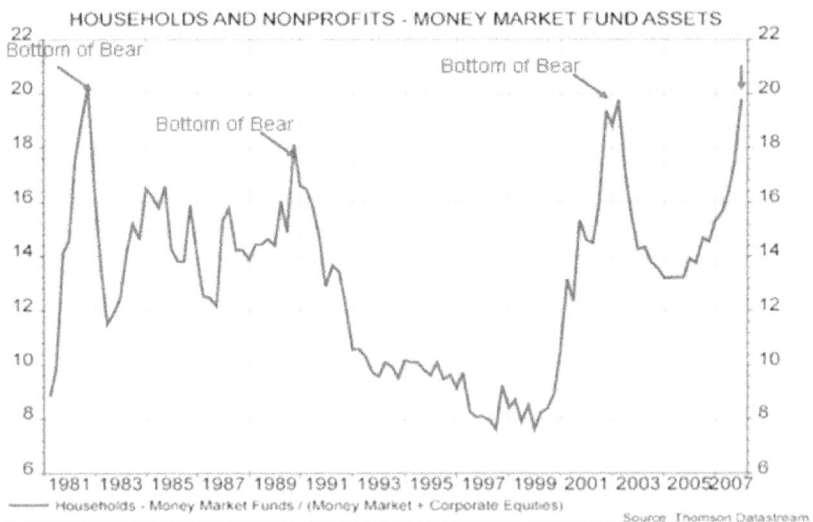

HOUSEHOLDS AND NONPROFITS - MONEY MARKET FUND ASSETS

As this data provided by Hays Advisory Services (March 2008) suggests, we are observing levels of cash so extreme that these heights have only been reached at the bottoms of bear markets last seen over the last 27 years. Eventually all this cash will serve as a tremendous mountain of fuel to power the market higher. With interest rates so low, once an economic recovery is anticipated, there will be tremendous amounts of white powder to drive equities higher. The chart below from Yardeni Research drives home the same point. There are a lot of skittish investors on the sidelines waiting to get back in the market.

The fearful public has now amassed more than $7.3 trillion of low yielding cash.

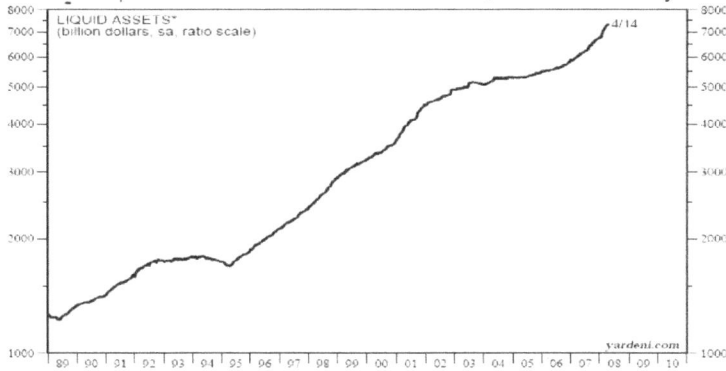

When is the exact time to get back in? It is effectively impossible to determine the precise time to bob in and out of markets. Or as Robert Rubin articulated in his book *In an Uncertain World,* "Nothing is certain – except uncertainty." However, one thing I am certain of after following the market for a few decades, managing a $20 billion fund, launching a hedge fund, and establishing my own investment firm (Sidoxia

Capital Management, LLC), if you follow your passions and dreams with an unrelenting determination, virtually anything is possible.

I congratulate you on completing my first book and wish you the best in the management of your financial future.

Sincerely,

Wade W. Slome

Wade W. Slome, CFA, CFP®

Appendix: *Balancing Professional & Personal Life*

Achieving balance in one's life is very important to me, whether talking about the balance between work and family or the balance between body, mind, and spirit. This appendix section is designed to show you a few examples of how I have strived to maintain balance in my life.

Bloomberg.com

American Century Ultra's Wade Slome Completes Mt. Whitney Climb

2005-08-08 17:02 (New York)

By Sophie Hayward

Aug. 8 (Bloomberg) -- Wade Slome, manager of American Century's $22 billion Ultra Fund, made it to the top of Mt. Whitney in California in 11 1/2 hours, some three hours less than he expected.

Slome completed the first major mountain climb of his life three days ago, equipped with hiking boots, walking poles and an iPod blasting rock 'n' roll for motivation.

"I was pushing to get up and down as fast as I could," he said. Slome credited training and an Advil tablet every few hours for pain management as keys to his success in climbing the 14,500-foot mountain.

The 35-year-old, who has managed Ultra for three years, took on the highest mountain in the continental U.S. with little climbing experience. He trained by running up and down the 16 flights of stairs at American Century's headquarters, where he works, and by walking on a treadmill at his home with a backpack full of dictionaries.

He was back at the office today, scarred only by sore calves. Slome, who climbed with his brother-in-law and his wife's uncle, encountered only one setback: a hail storm on the way down that he managed to walk through.

Slome is the second-youngest manager among the 25 biggest actively managed U.S. stock funds. Brian Hanson, co-manager of the $23 billion Fidelity Blue Chip Growth Fund, is the youngest. Hanson was born in 1973.

The climb "was an incredible experience and something I can tell my grandchildren about," the fund manager said.

--Editors: Melloy, Fu.

Story illustration: For more on the American Century Ultra fund, see {TWCUX US <Equity> DES <GO>}. To compare the fund's return during the past five years with the Standard & Poor's 500 Index, type {TWCUX US <Equity> COMP M SPX <GO>}.

To contact the reporter on this story:
Sophie Hayward in New York at (1) (212) 617-3037 or Shayward2@bloomberg.net.

Appendix: Balancing Professional & Personal Life

Poker – A True Love

As if playing the market was not enough gambling, I have fallen in love with the game of poker. Just as in investing, poker blends the art of behavior with the science of numbers and probabilities. But truth be told, this is not gambling. As famous trader, Jesse Livermore, so aptly stated, "A professional gambler is not looking for long shots, but for sure money." Adding strength to my argument is the performance of professional poker player, Dan Harrington. Dan Harrington finished in third place during the World Series of Poker Main Event in 2003. There were 839 participants, placing Mr. Harrington in the top 1/2 of 1% and earned him $650,000 that year. The following year, Mr. Harrington entered the same tournament; but due to the explosion in popularity, the number of participants had tripled. Nonetheless, "Action Dan" amazingly ended up finishing in fourth place (or in the top 1/4 of 1% of the participants), netting him $1.5 million in winnings. Odds, if left to chance, would be 1 in 25,000 for making the final table for both 2003 and 2004.

More recently, Greg Raymer, the winner of the main event in the 2004 World Series of Poker (with over 2500 participants), also proved that there is more than luck involved in the sport. The following year, Raymer ended up finishing 25th in the WSOP Main Event in a field of more than 5,600 players – putting him in the top ½%. Joe Hachem, the 2005 World Series of Poker winner, pulled off a slightly less incredible feat the following year when, in a pool of 8,800 players, (a 10x increase in participants over a three year period), Mr. Hachem finished in the #238 spot (a top 3% finish).

Bond Guru and fixed income portfolio manager at PIMCO (Pacific Investment Management Company), Bill Gross, has taken many of the lessons that he learned as a professional blackjack player in Las Vegas and applied them to making money as a professional bond manager. After living for a brief period in Las Vegas, he managed to turn $200 into $10,000 over a four month period. Mr. Gross uses a similar philosophy to counting cards when he invests in fixed income securities – when the odds and cards are stacked in his favor, then he invests a larger portion of his portfolio in those securities. As long as proper portfolio management techniques are used (i.e. do not risk your whole bankroll) and bets are spread out (diversified), then your odds of achieving success are much higher. Investing in stocks is no different. Success is never guaranteed; however, when extensive research creates favorable investment probabilities, then it only makes sense to invest a larger sum of money to exploit that financial edge. I follow the same line of thinking as I constantly rank my portfolio universe – I invest more of my money in stocks that have higher expected return profiles (better probabilities) and sell or own smaller percentages of stocks with lower or negative return profiles.

Walter "Puggy" Pearson hammered the nail on the head when he identified the three keys of professional gambling (and I argue investing) as, "Knowing the 60-40 end of a proposition, money management, and knowing yourself." Here again, a master of his craft has distilled a money-making strategy down to a mixture of art and science. The 60-40 aspect of risking capital represents the "science" facet and knowing yourself, the "art" component (money management I view as a mixture of the two).

My formal introduction to the game of No Limit Texas Hold'em poker resulted from a meeting with world champion Phil Hellmuth Jr. in 2003, and my infatuation with the sport continues with the same vigor today. Here is a brief Dow Jones article touching on that experience.

TIP SHEET: American Century Ultra's Slome Shuffles Cards

By Desiree J. Hanford Of DOW JONES NEWSWIRES 867 words 20 January 200414:00Dow Jones News ServiceEnglish(c) 2004 Dow Jones & Company, Inc.

ST. LOUIS (Dow Jones)--Managing the $23.8 billion American Century Ultra fund, for portfolio fund manager Wade Slome, is a little bit like playing poker.

But investors shouldn't be alarmed by that.

Slome's approach isn't that of the type of poker player who is trying to maximize short-term performance. That strategy might work for a while, but poker is a game of skill that requires longer-term thinking for success.

"Poker players don't wander and that's how they end up at the final table," said Slome, who beat award-winning poker player Phil Hellmuth Jr. at a hand of poker in August while Slome was attending a conference in Vail, Colo. "We stick to our process. We're looking to provide superior returns over the long-term basis."

The fund's returns show that Slome has been successful in doing that. American Century Ultra has lost an annualized 0.59% during the past five years through Jan. 15, ranking it 72 among the 320 large-cap growth funds tracked by Lipper Inc. The fund's peers have lost an annualized 3.12% during that time.

The fund has returned an annualized 8.77% during the past decade, compared with 7.55% for its peers. That ranks American Century Ultra 25 out of 92 large-cap growth funds.

Slome uses a bottom-up approach in finding stocks that have accelerating sales and earnings growth "because we think price follows earnings," he said.

"Because we're trying to look around the corner, not (at) the rearview mirror, we're also trying to understand if the acceleration is sustainable," Slome said. "Under the ideal scenario, we're trying to find the next Amgen (AMGN) or Starbucks (SBUX). What you get with those are compounding effect of earnings."

Slome thinks American Century Ultra has some of those types of stocks in its 150 or so holdings. InterActiveCorp (IACI) is one of them. The company is a play on Slome's expectation that more than 50% of total travel revenue will come from online usage by 2010, up from 15%, or $24 billion, in 2002.

It's also a play on the proliferation of broadband, a trend Slome expects to continue.

"It's amazing how much more time people spend on the computer when they have broadband," he said.

Shares of Interactive, one of Ultra's top 10 holdings on Nov. 30, closed at $34.88 Friday, up 88 cents.

There are several other technology stocks in American Century Ultra's top offerings, unlike in 2001 and 2002 when the sector's weighting was in the single digits on a percentage basis because technology earnings were anemic.

But going into 2003, Slome saw a "perfect storm" - low interest rates, a tax cut, improving corporate profits, consumers spending remaining robust - coming together and benefiting technology and Internet companies. Technology stocks accounted for half of the fund's top 10 holdings on Nov. 30, and the sector's weighting was 24.36% on Dec. 31.

Intel Corp. (INTC) was Ultra's largest holding at 2.92% at the end of November. Dell Inc. (DELL) was third at 2.73%, Microsoft Corp. (MSFT) fifth at 2.58% and Cisco Systems Inc. (CSCO) was sixth at 2.38%.

Slome finds Intel attractive for several reasons, including its Centrino mobile technology, which provides wireless Internet access. Other reasons include increased demand, improving prices, new technology and improved server sales. Those trends, combined with increased market share, are good news for Intel's margins and earnings, Slome said.

Intel's stock closed Friday at $32.89, down 17 cents.

Although there were concerns about Cisco's positioning in the telecom arena and competition from Asia, the company's response was to invest in new areas, including security, storage, and voice over Internet protocol, Slome said. That helped Cisco's margins increase and earnings improve. The signs that companies are starting to spend money again will help Cisco's results, Slome added.

Cisco closed Friday at $29.13, up $1.97.

Dell doesn't have the margins that Cisco has, but it is competitive on prices and it is getting into new markets such as printers, servers and storage, Slome said. Investors will hear more about Dell's consumer electronics strategy, an area where it can use its cost advantages, he added.

"We think you'll continue to see Dell grow above industry growth rates and gain market share," Slome said.

Dell closed Friday at $35.01, up 13 cents.

Given his appreciation for poker, perhaps it isn't surprising that another stock that Slome likes is gaming machine maker International Game Technology (IGT). The company is benefiting from more states allowing gambling, particularly as they attempt to increase revenue to offset rising expenses. International Game has a 70% market share, which allows it pricing power and the cash to repurchase shares and pay dividends, Slome said.

International Game's stock closed Friday at $35.64, up 24 cents.

-By Desiree J. Hanford, Dow Jones Newswires; 314-588-8443; desiree.hanford@dowjones.com

70715

Document DJ00000020040120e01k000hd

Appendix: Balancing Professional & Personal Life

Author Training Wheels

CORNELL BUSINESS

Johnson Graduate School of Management

Volume XX -4   December 11, 1996

Old Ezra Trip to Boston a Success!

by Wade Slome

While every MBA student has probably heard of the annual "Week on Wall Street" festivities held in New York City, many students have no clue what the "Walk Down State Street" event is all about. About 20 1st year Johnson students pounded the pavement (cold pavement I might add) through downtown Boston last week, visiting various buy-side and sell-side firms. Thanks to a few motivated second year students that originated the idea last year, the Old Ezra sponsored event celebrated its second successful State Street tour. Over the short two years of its existence, "Walk Down State Street" has resulted in visits to firms including; Fidelity Management & Research, Massachusetts Financial Services, Putnam Investments,

Wellington Management, John Hancock Advisors, Brown Brothers Harriman, Adams Harkness Hill, and more. Investment professionals and alumni from these firms spoke to the Johnson students about the flavor of the investment management industry as well as their day-to-day experiences.

After learning some Stock Market rap, the Old Ezra field-trippers chowed down some not so appetizing fish at the Boston Securities Analyst Society meeting and heard some local analysts speak about the HMO industry. The busy schedule of financial fun did not end there, as the group then hiked their way to an alumni reception at the Essex Grille

to enjoy some conversation and beer with former Johnson students.

Although none of the firms visited handed out summer internships, the students found the two day trip a an interesting way of learning more about the investment field and networking with alumni. "It was great to interact with alumni while at the same time learning more about the research analysis industry," commented Wade Slome, a first year student.

As a side note, if you're ever in Boston without your only pair of suit pants, I can recommend a place where you can buy a tailored suit ready to wear within 2 hours.

> Gotta love a quote by me in my own article!

CLASS OF 1998

CORNELL UNIVERSITY
Johnson Graduate School of Management

Wade W. Slome
M.B.A. Class of 1998

100 Fairview Square, #2G
Ithaca, NY 14850
Tel: 607 277-7761
e-mail: wws2@cornell.edu

Norris Road
Fremont, CA 94536
Tel: 510 793-

Slome, Wade William
Univ. of California - Los Angeles
William O'Neil @ Co. Ltd.
wws2@cornell.edu

YES, THAT IS MY
BIG NOGGIN' !

Soejarto, Alejandro D.
Univ. of Illinois - Urbana
Release International
ads20@cornell.edu

Song, Yan
Peking University

Spanswick, Robert John
Cornell University

Spence, Alexander L.
Univ. of Southern California

Spitzer, Andreas Mark
Virginia Tech

Appendix: Balancing Professional & Personal Life

Music – Food for the Soul

NO CAMERAS/RECORDERS
BILLY JOEL
THE 2000 YEARS TOUR
KEMPER ARENA
TUE DEC 7 1999 8:00 PM

ALL WEATHER EVNT
BUDWEISER TRUE MUSIC
LINKIN PARK/KORN/SNOOP
PROJEKT REVOLUTION 2004
VERIZON WIRELESS AMP-KC
IN ASSOC W/ MTV2/WRFF.COM
TUE AUG 24 '04 2PM DOORS

ticketmaster

KUP0425 GENADM GA6 172 A 22.50
ADMIT ONE PERSON
96.5 THE BUZZ PRESENTS
GENADM
MOBY
* * *
GA6 172 UPTOWN THEATER
3700 BROADWAY KCMO
A 6APRS MON APR 25 2005 7:00 PM

LIMITED VIEW
GOLDENVOICE PRESENTS
SOUNDGARDEN
* DANCE FLOOR ACCESS *
GRAND OLYMPIC AUDITORIUM
1801 S. GRAND

KA0401 225 0 2 A 34.00 EKA0401
BALCONY
98.9 THE ROCK PRESENTS
225
KID ROCK
* * *
MUNICIPAL AUDITORIUM
301 W 13TH ST KCMO
A23MAR THU APR 1 2004 7:30 PM

KUP0905 GA FLO GA7 102 A 52.50
GA FLOOR
* * * *
GA FLO ROBERT PLANT
AND STRANGE SENSATION
GA7 102 UPTOWN THEATER
3700 BROADWAY KCMO
A24JUN2 THU SEP 5 2002 8:00 PM

FLOOR GEN ADM ADULT
FLOOR
1 H ANNUAL BOB MARLEY
BIRTHDAY FESTIVAL
LONG BEACH ARENA
DOORS AT 1:00 PM
SAT FEB 13, 1993

KV0612 SEC 4 L 22 A 42.50 EKV0612
ALL WEATHER EVNT
* * *
PEARL JAM
WWW.PEARLJAM.COM
VERIZON WIRELESS AMPHTHR
$38/$34 + $4.50 FAC FEE
THU JUN 12 2003 7:30 PM

GEN AD GEN ADM ADULT
NO FLOOR ACCESS
GOLDENVOICE/MOSS JACOBS
PORNO FOR PYROS
RAIN OR SHINE
OLYMPIC VELODROME
CAL STATE DOMINGUEZ HILLS
SAT JUN 5, 1993 7:00 PM

PEARL JAM
RAIN OR SHINE/GATES AT 4P
EMPIRE POLO CLUB

KV0727 SEC 4 1 7 W 45.50 EKV0727
ALL WEATHER EVNT
* * *
SEC 4 JOHN MAYER
JOHNMAYER.COM/LOCAL-83.CO
VERIZON WIRELESS AMP-KC

PAL1015 GEN AD GEN ADM ADULT
GOLDENVOICE & AVALON PRES
BIG AUDIO DYNAMITE II
AT THE

Although these are not all the ticket stubs from concerts I have attended, they are somewhat representative samplings. Other notable concerts include my first concert in 3rd grade which was KISS (when they still wore make-up), The Who, U2, The Police, Tom Petty, among a host of 80s New-Wave bands.

Appendix: Balancing Professional & Personal Life

www.SlomeAdventure.Blogspot.com

In 2007, the Slome family had the pleasure of taking a 5,000+ mile RV trip that lasted 22 days. Here are a FEW excerpts from my blog (www.SlomeAdventure.Blogspot.com):

2007 RV Slome Adventure

2007 Winnebago 33' - a.k.a "The Beast"

Tuesday, May 8, 2007

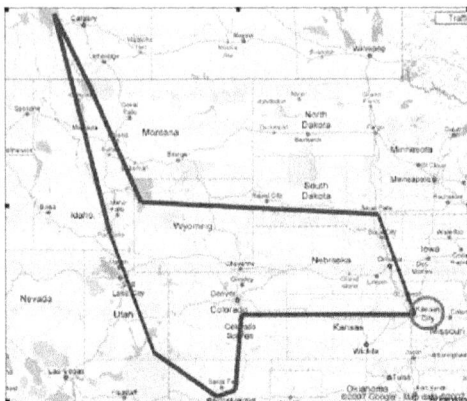

Slome-a-Palooza 2007

June 9th – June 30th (Stay tuned)

Saturday, June 9, 2007

AND THEY'RE OFF!!

6/9: During Day One the Slomes covered a respectable amount of territory, cutting through Nebraska, Iowa and eventually reaching our destination in Brandon, SD, just east of Sioux Falls. As a rookie RV-er, I give myself a passing grade on handling such an enormous vehicle without taking out any poles, pedestrians, or parked cars (thank God for insurance). Robin, my wingman/woman navigator, did a spectacular job entertaining Whitney and Hayley with minimal meltdowns. We ultimately arrived at Jellystone in one piece on the Beast's maiden voyage. We didn't run into Ranger Smith, but we did manage to get a family photo with Yogi as you can see. Hayley and Whitney had an enjoyable time at the Boo Boo Bubble Blowing contest before we settled back to the campsite for what Whitney called the "best smores that I've had in my whole life!" – O.K., Daddy will take some credit for that. Anyway, Day One is in the history books and we hope to follow in Yogi's footsteps and be smarter than the average bear as we continue on our journey. Tomorrow we head west towards Mt. Rushmore with a few interesting pit-stops along the way. Catch you next posting…

P.S. For those of you keeping score, the gas "Guzzle-meter" cashed in at $151.34 on the first day. Given that I started with a complementary full tank of 75 gallons, the bite of the first fill-up wasn't too bad. At 7 miles per gallon through the flat lands, I'm a bit worried what will happen to the Guzzle-meter through the mountains??!!

Monday, June 11, 2007
WOW, THOSE ARE SOME BIG HEADS

6/11: Day Three landed us at Mt. Rushmore. Besides just taking photos in front of the big heads, we also learned a few fascinating facts. First of all this sucker took fourteen years to carve to completion (Gutzon Borglum finished the spectacle in 1941). Named after Charles E. Rushmore, a lawyer living in the Black Hills in the late 1800s, who researched mining claims of local mining companies. Other tidbits include the fact that each head stands six stories tall and Abe Lincoln's mole measures sixteen inches. You can just call me the Cliff Claven of granite monuments.

Monday, June 11, 2007

WANTED...AND POTENTIALLY DANGEROUS

6/11: Local Authorities posted the following notice..."Two young females, aged 2 and 5 last seen boozing it up at the Mangy Moose Saloon in Hill City, South Dakota with some suspicious drifters that look rather worn out (we think they could be the parents). Crime committed is Kool Aid and chocolate ice cream theft from the Cactus Hill, South Dakota BP gas station. Our law enforcement agency has pictures of the suspects and accomplices posted statewide – a reward will be provided for any tips leading to the arrest of the suspects. Authorities remain unsure whether suspects are armed, but we know them to be factually crazy as evidenced by their twenty-three day RV trip."

Tuesday, June 12, 2007
SHOWER AT THE TOWER

6/12: And we needed a shower after a few days on the RV (ha). I have to admit there was a little Close Encounters déjà vu when we got to Devil's Tower. Team Slome, with their fortitude as usual, braved the elements (hooded jackets and all) to see this very abnormal looking mountain formation standing 5,100 feet tall. The story goes that an Indian girl drank some bear potion, turned into a bear, and then went on an attempted killing rampage of her sisters. Magical buffalo came to the rescue of the siblings by placing the kids on a flat rock that grew into the sky. In an effort to kill the siblings, the bear /sister clawed her way along the sides of the mountain, thus forming Devil's Tower. I may have gotten some of the story points wrong, but I think you get the gist.

In the spirit of a bear story, I can attest to the fact that today was a 'bear' of a travel day as well. Although the cross-state mountainous drive across Wyoming afforded us incredible views of towering bluffs, magnificent lakes, and picturesque river valleys – nonetheless spending 10+ hours maneuvering the Beast through hairpin turns accompanied by screaming kids dampened the splendor a tad.

Tomorrow we'll cruise around the Grand Tetons and surrounding lakes before heading to Yellowstone. 'Til next time…

***Guzzle-meter = $704.32 (I can feel Al Gore cringing, but we're only 4 days in.)P.S. Late posting because no WiFI connection at the Grand Tetons RV Campground.

Tuesday, June 12, 2007
YELLOWSTONE - OLD FAITHFUL

6/14: They should call Old Faithful, "Old Fume-ful" judging by the bathroom odors spewed from the countless geysers and dozens of other geological orifices (hot springs, mud pots, and fumaroles) covering the surrounding area. Or as Hayley blurted, "P.U. Daddy, stinky smell." Nonetheless, we muscled through the aromas to arrive at the main attraction (Old Faithful) and she didn't disappoint. At 1:58 p.m. the eruption began about one minute past the estimated blast time, and lasted the typical three to four minutes. The average height of the water eruption reaches 130 feet and temperatures around 200 degrees Fahrenheit. The 92 minute standard interval between eruptions allowed us time to take in all the other hydrothermal formations in the vicinity.

Before going on to our next adventure, Chef Robin whipped up an RV microwave special for our hungry munchkins before moving on to our next adventure.

Friday, June 15, 2007

THE BEAST IS BUSTED!!

"Things that were hard to bear are sweet to remember"
-Seneca - Roman philosopher, mid-1st century AD

6/15: The Beast has suffered a bum wheel – literally. It started off so innocently. Robin: "Wade, aren't you worried about the smoking back wheels? I don't think that's normal. " Wade: "Nahh, it's fine. The brakes are just a little tired from all the mountain driving we've done… don't worry." Famous last words.

Little did we know that we were undergoing a serious rear Axle Seal Differential problem (but of course), dumping quarts of oil through the South Dakota and Wyoming mountains. If untreated, we realized that the rear wheels could grind to a halt or worse yet result in the loss of brake power (gulp). Fortunately, Andrew from Yellowstone Park Service Stations (legs shown in above photo) filled up our injured vehicle with some 80/W90 Heavy Differential Lube and we limped our way to Bozeman, Montana (~135 miles) - leaving a nice grease slick souvenir for those we left behind. We did our best to ignore the incessant well-intentioned warnings from ongoing drivers and those nature observers covering their mouths from the foul smoke. Needless to say, we're alive and in one piece living large at the Best Western Gran Tree with our new "Beast-Lite" or "Beast-ette" (See below). The good Lord willing, M & W Repair will be able to fix the Beast tomorrow and we will be back on our trail? As always, pending WiFi accessibility, we will keep you posted…

Monday, June 18, 2007

HAPPY FATHER'S DAY!

6/17: The day started off grandly. Robin let me sleep in, then the kids greeted me with a "Happy Father's Day" hug, handed me a card, and gave me the ceremonial dad's day clothes and breakfast bear claw. After a warm embrace from Robin, she nonchalantly delivered my worst nightmare in a short but sweet fashion, "By the way Wade, the toilet's backed up." Inwardly panicked, outwardly calm, I tried to calculate my alternatives. Without getting into graphic detail, I decided to take the problem head on (no pun intended). With surgical gloves and coat-hanger in hand, I came to an unsuccessful resolution. The backup plan: outsource the problem to someone else as the Slomes usually do. Unfortunately, Sunday mornings on a holiday are not the best days to find hired help. The best I could do was find an on-call handyman two towns away who charged $125/hr + costs for travel time (that could be a time consuming and costly answer). Terror was beginning to set in. Time was ticking and the smell was building. What to do? Try your retired veteran RV neighbor who retired twenty years ago and lives in his coach – surely he'll have an answer. "I've never seen that in my life," he casually commented. Wonderful, I thought. "Have you tried a stick?" he suggested. Aha! It was genius - a simple but elegant solution. My high school Physics course confirmed that not only would I get a better grip but also better leverage in dealing with the issue at hand. His words of wisdom worked, and I was once again a happy father. The lesson to be learned: "stick"-to-it-iveness really does work.

Our plumbing delay did cut our Lewis & Clark tour short. The "Gates of the Mountains" in Montana is a small slice of Meriwether Lewis' and William Clark's 8,000 mile trip from St. Louis to the Pacific and back (1804-1806). Thomas Jefferson commissioned the men to explore the newly acquired Louisiana Purchase to see if there was a waterway to the Pacific Ocean.

Wednesday, June 20, 2007

FLYING HIGH

Flying high were the Slomes on Day 11 (mentally and physically) as we reached the halfway point of our trip. After being cooped up for a day due to rain, Mother Nature accommodated us with some splendid weather this morning before our long drive to Canada. Us adrenaline junkies took advantage of the conditions and jumped on a Glacier Heli Tour of the park. We didn't require the use of sanitation bags, but the thought crossed our minds when we were being thrown around like rag dolls at 10,000 feet. Regardless, the spectacular views made up for any queasiness we experienced.

Thursday, June 21, 2007

TOTO, WE'RE NOT IN KANSAS

6/20: It's days like today that I really need to pinch myself to remind me that we're not back home in Overland Park, Kansas. Well O.K., we don't have any soaring mountains or rich colored emerald glacial lakes there, but we do have a world class petting zoo (Deanna Rose for the non-locals) and a kick-butt SuperTarget. Even so, I manage the drudgery of pulling out the camera for yet another breath-taking view. Besides cultivating the camera eye of an Ansel Adams, I've also developed the back of an ox from lugging Hayley's 30 lbs (and change) on each of our adventures. Look for me on the next ESPN heavy truck pulling challenge (Robin & kids will be touring with me on the Winnebago).

The photo above is the Slome gang hanging out at Lake Louise (named after Princess Louise Caroline Alberta [1848-1939] – daughter of Queen Victoria of England). The remarkable emerald coloring of the lake is a result of light-absorbing silt deposited primarily by the Lefroy glacier. The silt soaks up all colors of the spectrum except for emerald green & blue. We truly lucked out with the weather since Lake Louise is often frozen from November to June and June weather is hit or miss (it rained all of last week).

Friday, June 22, 2007

SEA MONKEY TRAGEDY – DEATH BY WHEAT THINS

6/22: In order to acclimate Whitney's transition to her new home on wheels, we thought it would be a bright idea to bring along a pet companion. What better pet(s) than Sea Monkeys (related to Brine Shrimp)? Whitney's world came tumbling down like a house of cards when Daddy mistakenly executed the recommended oxygenation process (blowing bubbles into the aquarium with a straw). The only problem was that Daddy had just finished stuffing his fat face with Wheat Thins, and in the process accidentally spewed half chewed cracker floaties into the Sea Monkey surroundings. Oops. It wasn't a pretty sight to watch at that point – the poor little monkeys proceeded to gorge themselves to a gluttonous death. Given the circumstances, the girls handled it fairly well, as seen by the ornate burial ceremony shown below. Carefully hand picked flowers, rocks, and leaves were laid at the Sea Monkey cemetery (Hayley's right foot).

(Whitney & Hayley's Sea Monkey Burial Ceremony)

Monday, June 25, 2007

SHIZER SANITIZER

6/24: A few days have passed since we last spoke about our potty issues in the "Beast", so plug your noses again. In order to honor a previous pledge to a friend, I feel obligated to share the joy of my daily ritual...RV waste removal. (This one's for you, Kenny G.)

What better way to spend your morning, than cleaning out the crapper (debate still exists whether Thomas Crapper [1836-1910] invented the flushing toilet, but his patent for the 'symphonic flush' remains uncontested). Diaper duty for Whitney, and now Hayley, did little to prepare me for the vital soil cleansing duties needed for our RV adventure. The precision of a surgeon is required, as can be seen from my protective gear. From the layman's view the mechanics appear straightforward, but the reality is that one false move can prove lethal. Behind the curtains of the brown hose (appropriately colored and shown above), lies pulleys, pumps, valves, black and grey water meters, sewage caps and more. Fortunately the nervous adrenaline along with the brisk stench, which acts as a smelling salt, has kept me on my 'A' game - thus preventing any major misstep from occurring. You can ask Robin about the infamous Day Three incident offline. After all is said and done, and the sweet gurgling sound of expulsion is heard, I then know my mission has been accomplished.

I'm now pooped out from talking about this subject, so if you want any more details you can contact me when I get back. There you go, Ken, my obligation has now been fulfilled.

ROCK N" IN UTAH

6/24: Hole, sweet hole. Now we experienced how life would be for the Flintstones in Bedrock. 'Hole N" The Rock' pretty much sums it up. Some neurotic guy named Albert Christensen, a jack of all trades (miner, taxidermist, accountant, artist, barber, chef), decided to hand-chip a 5,000 square foot home (14 rooms) inside a rock and operate a diner out of his kitchen. The project took 20 years and he only lived in it for five before he died in 1957 at the age of fifty-four. Today, besides the living hole area, Hole N" the Rock is also home to an eclectic set of attractions including a trading post, petting zoo, FDR memorial, tin statues, souvenir shops, and more.

(One of the rooms in the Christensen's hole-home).

Tuesday, June 26, 2007

DINNER IS SERVED –

THE ULTIMATE IN FINE RV DINING

6/25: This evening's menu consisted of the best that Western American cuisine can offer, including: delectable peas and carrots sautéed in a light butter sauce (Del Monte), hearty flambéed beef frank (Hebrew national) in bun, complemented by baked cheddar crisps (Cheetos), chilled Apple-Strawberry-Banana fruit purée (Mott's), sparkling raspberry beverage (Diet Rite soda), and topped off with a divine chocolate pastry and vanilla ice cream bar (Blue Bunny) for dessert. Just a little "heaven on earth" [beautifully presented on Day 2 Corn Palace placemat] for our RV bellies to sustain us through the last leg of our journey.

DESERT DELIGHT

6/25: Delicate Arch is the most widely-recognized landmark in Arches National Park (Moab, UT) and is depicted on both Utah license plates and a postage stamp commemorating Utah's centennial anniversary of statehood in 1996. The Olympic torch relay for the 2002 Winter Olympics passed through the arch. Initially our three-mile hike sounded manageable, that was until one factored in the steep mountain grade, blistering heat in the 90s, and the lugging of two under-aged kids. Nonetheless, we persevered and survived (barely) to soak in some of the wildest and most breathtaking rock formations we've ever seen. Arches National Park preserves over 2,000 natural sandstone arches made primarily from unique Entrada sandstone but also some from Navajo sandstone. The national park lies atop an underground salt bed, which is the main cause of the formation of the arches and spires, balanced rocks, sandstone fins, and eroded monoliths that were created millions of years ago and continue to transform today. Water, frost, and wind have carved these enormous but graceful arches, windows, spires, and pinnacles. The park was a lot larger than I expected (~119 square miles in size) as it took us a good 45 minutes not including our two and half hour hike. Mission accomplished, next stop Albuquerque, New Mexico.

Saturday, June 30, 2007

'FATIGUE' HAS SET IN

6/29: Too many Winnie the Pooh DVD repeats? Mosquito contracted West Nile symptoms? Perhaps all the microwaved corn dogs and chicken nuggets have now exerted a toll? Or maybe it's just one too many 400 mile drives? Irrespective of the cause, there are no worries now that we are just a short 175 mile jaunt from Salina to our home base Mecca.

I think it was Vince Lombardi who said, "Fatigue makes cowards of us all," but as far as I'm concerned fatigue just makes me sleepy. When I get back from the trip, I'm recommending Winnebago design a pillow feature right into the steering wheel. Fortunately the screaming kids and caffeinated beverages prevented me from driving the Beast straight off a cliff.

Sunday, July 1, 2007

THANKS AND FAREWELL. UNTIL NEXT TIME...

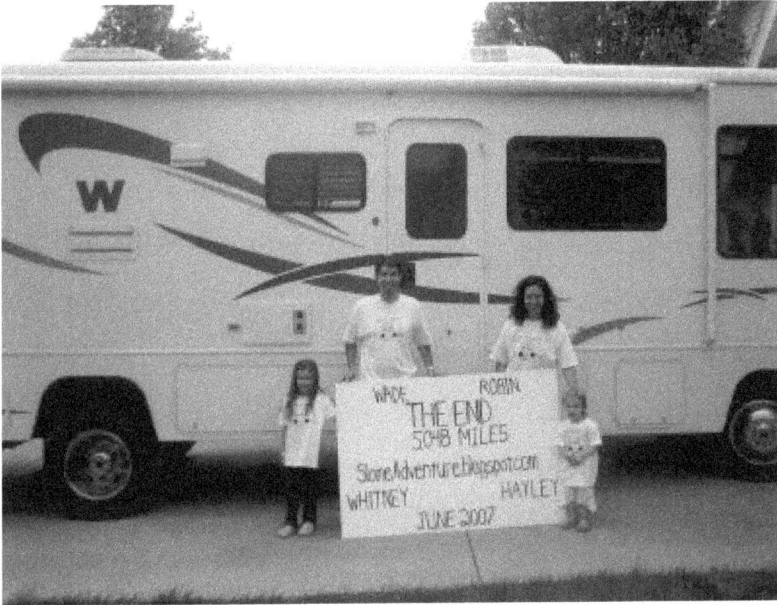

6/30 (Day 22 - Final Day):

In the great immortal words of Jerry Garcia, "What a long, strange trip it's been." An unforgetably fun one at that.

Thank you to all the faithful blog followers whose phone calls, e-mails, and blog postings have made this such a memorable trip. Unbeknownst to many, 'Big Brother' was watching the anonymous blog viewings at SlomeAdventure.blogspot.com via traffic meter software we installed on our laptop halfway through the trip. To our surprise, interest steadily built and peaked at 327 daily page views, with at least people in four countries periodically peeking. Although no Google equivalent, as far as site traffic goes, the blog still gave us the voyeuristic opportunity to track site interest.

Returning alive with all limbs after covering an extensive 5,048 miles journey like this engenders a great deal of gratitude to both people and aspects of the trip that we couldn't fully describe in a relatively short daily entry. So in a laundry list format, here are some of the people/things that deserve further recognition:

-Robin (Editor-in-Chief of blog, along with Vice President of RV Kid Management)

-Hospitable hosts (i.e. Schullers, Magnussens, Jenkins, Tomlinsons, Schipfers, among others)

-Dodie & Norm (for all their postings)

-DVD Player (Digital crack for the kids)

-Garmin GPS Device (Our guide-dog for the blind)

-SiteMeter (Our 'Big Brother' software)

-Deodorant (Active bodies will perspire)

-Stick (See day eight of blog)

-Fruit Snacks (Hayley's heroin)

-Double Smores (Whitney's invention)

-WiFi (For without this our blog would not be possible)

-Baseball Hats (Bed-head mitigation)

-Boo-Boo Kitty (Pink cat-shaped ice pack for RV adventure bumps/bruises)

-Books on Tape (Ace on the River – Barry Greenstein; A little

History of the World – E.H. Gombrich; and Grammar Girls
Quick & Dirty Tips – Mignon Fogarty)

-iPod (For mind-numbing 400 mile drives)

-Con Te Partiro (Andrea Bocelli – morning music to soothe the savage beasts)

-Toilet sanitizer (Self explanatory)

Thanks again to all the blog-ees and we will look forward to documenting our adventures in the future. Perhaps we will see you next year....for Slome Adventure 2008???

-WS

Acknowledgements

Special thanks go out to Dan Block, Ken Gau, Kirk Ridgway, and Heather Pierce for removing the rough edges off of this coarse piece of work. I appreciate the digital pencil and eraser skills they openly offered by editing this project from all corners of the United States (Northwest, Midwest, and East coast).

www.ingramcontent.com/pod-product-compliance
Lightning Source LLC
Chambersburg PA
CBHW031404180326
41458CB00043B/6612/J